END

In his book, *Rebuilding the Broken Altar*, Greg Hood presents a masterpiece of hope for the future of the church, for America and for nations crying out for a move of God. He carefully, biblically and prophetically lays out a blueprint for revival that every leader and believer alike can work with to shift culture and engage the spiritual atmosphere to bring change. The word studies bring incredible insight and reveal the important elements necessary for rebuilding the altar of the Lord which has been broken down in both the church and in society in order to see an unprecedented outpouring from heaven, harvest and transformation. In this tipping point moment of history, believers cannot afford to give in to hopelessness, complacency, fear or despair but must rise to the challenge to turn a nation back to God. This book will inspire you with the understanding that God has not abandoned America, but rather, our greatest days of fulfillment, demonstration and advancement for the Kingdom of God are still ahead. Thank you, Greg, for this magnificent charge to the Body of Christ to embrace our finest hour.

Dr. Jane Hamon, *Vision Church @ Christian International*

Author of: *Dreams and Visions, The Deborah Company, The Cyrus Decree, Discernment*

Rebuilding the Broken Altar is a key revelation to seeing the counterfeit altars dismantled and overthrown, and the manifest presence of the Lord established from region to region. Many have been praying, engaging in spiritual warfare, and working passionately, with great faith and hope, to see a mighty outpouring of Holy Spirit in revival and spiritual awakening, and yet we have not seen the fullness of the fires and glory of God's presence and power manifested that we see in Scripture or in previous moves of God throughout Church history. It is time for us as the people of God, the Ekklesia of the Lord, to engage in repairing the true Altar of the Lord.

Greg's keen prophetic gifting, strong apostolic authority, and solid foundation in the Word of God come through loud and clear in *Rebuilding the Broken Altar.* The clarity of revelation and practical application of how the Stones of the Altar, representing each of the Tribes of Israel, is vitally important for the days in which we are living. This is not simply a book to read, but a book of reference to be referred back to time and time again as we all endeavor to see the altar of the Lord restored in our own lives and in the territories to which God has assigned us.

Thank you, Apostle Greg, for investing your life in God's purposes and for making this book available to us all!

For His Glory,

Jacquie Tyre, Apostolic Leader, Kairos Transformation Ministries – CityGate Atlanta

Greg has laid out a clear directive on Rebuilding the Broken Altars that are much needed presently. Greg draws truth to a fine point. The sharpened edge you will find on these pages can become truth to make you free. His revelation will surely usher you into a greater level of spiritual understanding. Greg through and prophetic gifting and teaching flare enhanced by a kingdom heart to equip the Body of Christ has surely hit a home run here. Enjoy, grow and expect God to reveal himself on a greater level to you.

Clay Nash, Author of *Activating the Prophetic, Relational Authority,* and *God Dreams to Make America Great Again*

I just finished perusing *Rebuilding the Broken Altar*. WOW! What a timely revelatory prophetic book for today! I personally endorse this book as one of the most significant revelations for every five-fold minister, apostle, prophet, teacher, evangelist, pastor and every leader in the church. Read it, practice it, and watch the power of God using His gifted church for His ultimate intentions. The devil lost and God won, that will be the headlines in the next seasons.

Greg Hood has come as an apostle to the kingdom for such a time as this. He's a man of prayer, he has apostolic power and he's a leader among leaders. God bless all who read this book. It's a life changer.

Apostle Emanuele Cannistraci, Founding Pastor of GateWay City Church, San Jose, CA

Greg Hood's book, *Rebuilding the Broken Altar*, unfolds like a map on a road trip across the country. From his detailed examination of each of the 12 tribes of Israel and how they impact us today, Greg takes us effortlessly from the deeds of the ancients to the needs of modern culture as we watch from the windows of our Winnebago, content to pull off here and there as our interests are piqued.

Greg presents such a varied landscape that, if you don't like what he's saying in one paragraph, stay seated and go on to the next.

These pages are a wonder to behold. I highly recommend spending a few days with this magnificent tome.

Dr. Harold R. Eberle, Worldcast Ministries, Author of *Father-Son Theology*

My friend Greg Hood is known as hard-hitting, straight-shooting and uncompromising in his preaching. His writing is even more so! I love the way he boldly challenges us to break free from old religious mindsets so that we can embrace God's kingdom plans. In his new

book *Rebuilding the Broken Altar*, Greg gives us a clear vision of a restored church. With rich insights about the twelve tribes of Israel, he takes us on a journey toward the restoration of New Testament faith. You will be challenged and inspired!

J. Lee Grady, Author and Director of The Mordecai Project

The prophetic voice is blown from the Shofar by our dear brother Greg Hood to remind us that *Rebuilding the Broken Altar* is the order of the time. He helps us to understand the meaning of the time and grasp the seismic impact of the altar. I have had the privilege of Greg's friendship and the blessings of his clear prophetic voices. I praise the Lord Jesus for enabling him to write this valuable book.

Tamrat Layne, Former Prime Minister, Ethiopia

I believe this timely book will challenge you to your purpose on planet earth. Greg has hit the nail on the head as he encourages us to rebuild the altar. Greg has a passion to see God's kingdom established on earth as it is in heaven. This book will cause the sleeping giant in you to rise up and take its place. It will change how you view scripture!

Neil Miers, pastor & founder of Global Connexions Church, Australia

Dr. Greg Hood's book, *Rebuilding the Broken Altar*, is full of spiritual insights. It will inspire you to a closer walk with God! I have known him for over a Decade as having a powerful and distinct Holy Spirit's anointing upon his life and ministry.

Dr. David A Sobrepena, Word of Hope Church, Manila, Philippines

It's amazing to see that there's still hope and the church holds the key to bring forth a move of God to this world which desperately needs it. This is why it's very refreshing to find men like Greg Hood writing *Rebuilding the Broken Altar* at a time when the church needs a GPS to get back to its first love. I'm so thankful that my good friend continually thirsts for God's righteousness. Greg has cultivated profound spiritual insight which reveal biblical blueprints to building a living altar with a living God!

Alex Panetta, CEO, TBN PACIFIC Brisbane, Queensland, Australia

Rebuilding the Broken Altar by Greg Hood is a "now" prophetic message for the Church, and Church leaders. Each stone used to rebuild the altar represents one of the 12 Tribes of Israel. As Greg unpacks the rich metaphor and prophetic application for us today, it will fill you with hope and a holy zeal for His Kingdom.

I love this book! Every serious student of God's Word will love this book! It is a goldmine of revelation and prophetic understanding for this hour. Greg Hood has an amazing prophetic voice for this day!

Faylene Sparkes, Director, Australian Company of Seers

The Lord Jesus was fond of using the phrase, "those who have ears to hear, let them hear." He was indicating that what He was saying at the time, held deep spiritual truth that would require knowledge and wisdom to discern, and maturity to apply.

This is precisely what we find in Dr. Greg Hood's most recent book, *Rebuilding the Broken Altar*. The Holy Spirit of God has revealed to Dr. Hood intensely relevant and timely truths using prophetic and priestly symbolism (the altar and the breastplate), which the writer presents to us, in a fascinating, informative and comprehensive way. God intends the message of this book to heal, excite and empower his believers, his church and this nation, to repentance and power!

You won't want to put this book down. There is little doubt that Dr. Hood has an anointing for preaching. His spiritual gift is clearly manifested in his writing as well. In these pages, the deep truths of the Holy Spirit will call to the deepest parts of your soul and spirit (Ps 42:7), reigniting and fanning holy fire into a righteous inferno.

Dr. Wendell Choy, President, Ohana Christian Institute

Greg Hood has done an excellent job of presenting the history and relevance of the building of God's kingdom and structure in his book, *Rebuilding the Broken Altar*.

In this book, we find that God is revealing his plans for us. God is always doing a work in us to do a work through us. Partnering with God, listening to his voice, understanding the times and seasons we live in, are vital as we move forward in these days.

Greg has done an excellent job of "unpacking" truth and wisdom to help us align ourselves with God, move past all of the mistakes we've made and develop discernment and understanding of God's kingdom and building process in us. *Rebuilding the Broken Altar* is loaded with supernatural insight into some of the hidden mysteries that will realignment our thinking and give us solid instruction as we move forward in the days ahead.

Cindy McGill, Hope for the Harvest Ministries, Author of *What Your Dreams Are Telling You*

Altars of worship require assemble, order, and renewed covenant. The scattered stones say nothing, silent and waiting for the leader to whom their purpose is apparent. A thousand can walk around them without knowing their use, but a man of God on assignment can restore them in a day.

Greg Hood presents a prophetic picture of powerful perception: the stones of the wounded altar must be restored with covenant order, healed with consecrated hands, and renewed by God's fire.

Rebuilding the Broken Altar unpacks the significance of prophetic presentations of purpose, reveals the markers that make forgotten covenants functional, and set the proper order to worship. Missing even one stone can leave God's people off-target for his lightning.

Reset your own altar. Join the Remnant resetting the altars of nations. Become part of God's move to bring the scattered stones together for kingdom come, culture, and conquest in this generation.

Dr. Don Lynch, Ministry Matrix International, Jacksonville, FL

Greg's prophetic insights have been a great help in my spiritual life, giving practical guidance and confirming directions in my life. His sincerity and obvious love for Jesus filters through his deep revelation of God's word. Now you can also take part of his eye-opening revelations in the word. I strongly recommend this book.

Lars Brittsjo, CEO, Business Owner, Singapore

The Church is the hope of the World. Now more than ever our world and our Nation is grasping for hope. And now is the perfect storm for the church to arise and be that platform of hope. Apostle Greg Hood presents a Biblical strategy that will position the church to do just that. *Rebuilding the Broken Altar* challenges every believer to fixate ourselves on the one who is the source of all hope. It reminds us that God has created each of us for such a time as this. This book will awaken you to God's plan to usher in a Great Awakening.

Pastor Guy Kapeliela, God Squad Church, Oahu, Hawai'i

Apostle Greg Hood's new book, *Rebuilding the Broken Altar*, not only will stir your spirit, but Greg's spirit-inspired insights will light your path to discover your tribe and find your destiny. This book is a must-read for all who long to be actively involved in what God is doing on earth now and whose hearts burn to see "the kingdom of the world become the kingdom of our Lord"

Mike Henson, Pastor, Bethel Worship Center, Marion, Indiana

Using the twelve stones of the altar that Elijah built, representing the twelve tribes of Israel and their respective particular character traits, Greg Hood provides us a concrete tool of remembrance to help us apply Gods principles in our actions and lives in family, church and government, God's three institutions.

Greg Hood recognizes that we as individuals, leaders, parents, family and church are being challenged as never before. We are living in times the prophets of old spoke of. Wonderful, challenging and difficult times. The fire of God will come again on a much larger scale than He did on Elijah's altar. May we be prepared and active in bringing his will into as many peoples, families and nations as we possibly can.

Used as anchors of remembrance, Elijah's twelve stones with their respective tribal names explained, for inspiration and warning and guidance.

Cam Cavasso, Hawaii business owner, Former Hawaii State Representative

Rebuilding the Broken Altar is a Spirit-inspired battle cry for the heart and soul of our nation. As I read Greg's book with eyes of faith, I was encouraged with fresh hope for the future. The gift of the Apostle, whom God has given to the Church to reveal mysteries, will do that!

Greg's use of "stone imagery" to define the issues and strategies that will move us to have greater courage in this conflict of the ages is compelling. This revelatory work will help each of us to discover our own gifts and call so that we can be used as partners to repair God's altar -the place where God meets with man. When this happens and his holy fire falls on our nation, there is no telling how many lives will be touched, souls saved, and glory be given to God!

Terry Garrett, Lead Pastor, KingsGate Worship Center, Tupelo, MS

At a time when nations are trembling, economies are shaken, and news platforms stream uncertainty, Apostle Greg Hood brings a revelatory message that speaks truth to lies, order to chaos, come alive to dreams and hope to the future.

Rebuilding the Broken Altar engages you to look beyond circumstances and challenges you to discover and fully embrace God's plan for your life, city and nation. Present yourself and join me in earnest prayer and expectation, "Lord let your kingdom come your will be done on earth as it is in heaven and send your fire!"

Vicki Nohrden, Wind and Fire Ministries, Monterey, CA

Thank you, Apostle Greg, for your bravery in exposing your heart beating in union with Abba Fathers, into this book. Even though it's a prophetically inspired clarion call to all who would have "an ear to hear," it's so much more than that. This book is a reflection of the vision and desire contained in Greg's heart for people and nations to come into an awareness of how to see their lives and nations restored and used for God's glory and purposes.

So many of us pray, "Your kingdom come, Your will be done" but this book gives practical steps and instructions on how to start that process. By Rebuilding the Broken Altars of our personal lives and those of our nations, we better position ourselves to be led by Holy Spirit and used by our Father to achieve his kingdom purposes. A vital and very timely message for the season and age we live in.

Kevin Philippi, Business Owner, Queensland Australia

Dr. Hood's book is about a place where man meets God called an altar. He traces the pattern of Elijah Rebuilding the Broken Altar before the priests of Baal aka our rebuilding our relationship with God before anything worthwhile can be accomplished – mundane or miraculous. He says America's altar stones have been dismembered and dismantled and need to be returned to their proper place in unison as the 12 tribes of cover all the bases for Israel's well-being.

The bottom-line message of this book, God is not finished with you or America, but the church and some pastors and some of us in government need to get our stones together.

Representative Gene Ward, PhD, Hawai'i House of Representatives

In these times when Ethnos (culture) is raising against ethnos (culture), when God is being challenged in schools, universities, government, media and religious institutions, God is reclaiming his bride from religion and denominations to the Apostolic Ekklesia, so the Church can be his voice again and not an echo to the Nations.

Apostle Greg Hood captures the King's decree to the Church and the Nations. Time for passivity, compromise, perversion and religion is up. It's time to Repair and Rebuild according to God's order and pattern. I believe this book will stir up the Body of Christ globally to awaken her to her true identity and Purpose.

Pastor Newton Festus, Senior Pastor, Waterbrook Church Brisbane, Brisbane, Queensland Australia

Rebuilding the Broken Altar will bring back the FIRE of GOD where God intended his Presence to dwell on the altar of your heart "*A fire shall always be burning on the altar; it shall never go out*" Lev. 16:13

Apostle Greg's book is provocative, revelational, and intentional for such a time as this!

Dr. Virginia Domligan, BRS, The Prayer Center of the Pacific The Hawaiian Islands

In *Rebuilding the Broken Altar*, Dr. Greg Hood reaffirms God's plan to use our calling and giftedness as He establishes his kingdom on earth. In this transformational process, "There is a difference between God working in our midst and God working through us." Biblically, the altar is a sacred place to purify our motives, to receive our marching orders and the miraculous meets the mundane. At the altar of God, the ordinary becomes extraordinary, the mission becomes a mandate and transformation begins. Each of the 12 Stones Elijah used to rebuild the altar represents a profound message from a powerful messenger. Thank you, Dr. Hood, for reminding those who partner in God's kingdom work on earth, that the Lord's altar is both a place of prayer and the presence of God.

Dr. Greg Smith, Founder/President of InStep Global, Atlanta, GA

Greg Hood is a man with a clear understanding of the seasons and times we live in. His book has a clear-cutting edge in aligning God's church with his word, and in bringing great insight to us all.

Apostle Greg's revelation is profound in its delivery and draws a sharp line of commitment and obedience to prayer, especially in relation to these twelve altars.

Evangelist Alan Wills, Alan Will Ministries, Northlakes, Queensland, Australia

Apostle Greg Hood carries an authentic breakthrough revelatory apostolic ministry in this new epoch season for the restoration and restitution of God's people and the church.

In his new book, *Rebuilding the Broken Altar*, Apostle Greg Hood releases a powerful prophetic message bringing hope and truth which cuts through the many voices that are bringing chaos and confusion to many in the body of Christ.

Rebuilding the Broken Altar will empower you to receive fresh revelation and understanding to reset faulty foundations and establish divine alignment and divine order both in the church and in your personal lives.

The author, Greg Hood has set out with great skill and prophetic insight, detailed practical biblical truths we can apply in the rebuilding of our personal and corporate Altars

This book is an exciting read and a challenging resource in preparation for the greatest outpouring of the Holy Spirit into the earth. A "must-have resource."

Apostle Peggy Barr, Living Streams Apostolic Centre, Sunshine Coast, Queensland Australia

Rebuilding the Broken Altar is a word in season for the Church. Greg has a deep understanding of God's Word and its application to our lives today. You will be ready to jump to action after reading this book.

Jeremy and Emily Bell, Kingdom Entrepreneurs,
Brisbane, Queensland, Australia

In *Rebuilding the Broken Altar*, Greg has brought us back to the heart of the matter. Our God cut a covenant with His people that we would know Him and be like Him. The 12 stones reveal God's desire to

redeem our humanity and impart His divinity. Design reveals created purpose. We were made to know Him, unfiltered, uncorrupted from the lies and control of religion. Greg's apostolic passion for us to truly know God comes through strong and clear. So too does his warning, the great pretender and deceiver, religion, seeks to capture our hearts and minds in opposition to the knowledge of the true experienced knowledge of our God.

Through Rebuilding the Broken Altars Greg has prophetically brought to life again the apostolic foundation Jehovah put in our forefathers. As I read through the 12 real men that were the stones, I found myself reflected in their DNA and destiny. I can hear echoes of my identity and my purpose, and the call to be more in my generation.

Jeffrey Sparkes, Founder, Transform Corporate Services
Brisbane, Queensland, Australia

I met and encountered the ministry of Greg Hood in a very challenging time. Sitting and listening to his authentic and relevant teachings, I also had the sense of prophetic accuracy from his very first sentence. Not only was his word of knowledge about my life and ministry at that point in time exact, but the prophetic utterances offering guidance on the way forward brought so much clarity. He impressed me with his ability to connect with his listeners and I believe he will do the same with the readers of this book. Greg definitely has the ability to take obscure Biblical facts, expose their meaning, and apply it with great efficiency to inspire and enthuse God's people. Reading this manuscript, the words of Jesus come to mind that if you stop the people, the stones will cry out. Greg effectively takes the stones representing the tribes of Israel and lets them speak. The message emanating from the various stones, connects us in this current world and its challenges with the sons of Jacob, and brings the meaning of their names to life in a very unique way. As the spiritual and corporate leader of various ministries focusing on Biblical Worldview education, I am convinced that I can endorse Greg's prophetic exhortation with great confidence. I truly believe that many people will be blessed through his ministry and through this book.

Slabbert Pretorius (Lth, BA, Bth hons, Mth), Senior Pastor of Accelerate Church, Managing Director of Accelerate Educational Ministries, CEO of Southern Cross Educational Enterprises

It was my privilege to meet Greg Hood, through a mutual friend Robert Henderson, who has become known himself for his tremendous revelations on the Courts of Heaven, as well as other great books. Greg had by the grace of God, been given a revelation that concerned me and our church and came to our church to administer it. His gift was clear and his ministry clearly from God. As a result, we became friends and have ministered together on quite a few occasions.

Greg has a unique understanding of the times! And this book clearly shows it, I believe he is a modern-day, 'son of Issachar,' which is an absolute rarity within the days we live in. He preaches with clarity and now writes with the same clarity. I recommend this book and I recommend Greg. You will experience an awakening to God's ways and the way we should respond.

Dennis Goldsworthy-Davis, author of *Unlimited Anointing, Walking In The Prophetic*, and *Touching The God Of Jacob*.

I consider it a privilege and an honor to recommend Greg's newest book on the *Rebuilding the Broken Altar*. It's exciting to see men sharing the values of the Kingdom with such clarity and depth of understanding.

We live in a time when much of the world considers the church to be an antiquated moss backed Dinosaur with little relativity to a postmodern world. Greg shows in this work that he has a firm grasp on the hand of God moving through time to the restoration of all things. Many are the obsequious followers of escapist theology ready to relegate society and the earth to the enemy of our souls. I thank God for men like Greg who are willing to stand up and challenge us with the fact that we are anything but lost!

You will find a veritable cornucopia of teaching information within the pages of Greg's newest book. It has been a lost fact that Jesus spoke more of the Kingdom than any other subject in the Word of God. Instead of seeing us defeated by a waning societal caring for the Church, Greg sees the hand of God superintending all things for His glory. God is not even close to being finished with America or His people in her. We can take heart with the hope found in the pages of his book that will make you want to stand up proudly and say yes, there are still mighty men in the kingdom, for the spirit of the warrior and the mighty man of valor is still alive.

Thank you, Greg, for the years of prayer and diligent study as you were guided by the Holy Spirit to produce this timely work. May it truly be a blessing to all who enter its pages.

Paul A. Doherty, Ph.D, Th.D., founder, Victory Fellowship Church, Little Rock, Arkansas

The Bible says we are living stones, fit together to be a dwelling place for the Spirit of God. As Greg takes us through a study of Elijah rebuilding the Lord's altar with the 12 stones of the Tribes of Israel, we can see how important it is to take our place in the Body of Christ. As we each take our place, our "tribe position", we have the ability through God to bless and advance the Kingdom of God or to curse and delay or even stop the move of Holy Spirit. I encourage each of us to take this book and ask Holy Spirit to help us find our place and do our part in becoming those who are advancing the Kingdom and declaring "Your Kingdom come, your will be done on earth as it is in Heaven"!

Dr. John Benefiel, Heartland Apostolic Prayer Network - Presiding Apostle, Church on the Rock – Senior Pastor

In this timely book Apostle Greg Hood, whom I've known for 28 years and walked with through many highs and lows, shows us how to look at today's world through God's Kingdom perspective rather than the panic religion is promoting through current events. You must read this!

Bishop Murray Galloway, Home Front Network

For years I have been tremendously blessed by the ministry and friendship of Apostle Greg Hood. He walks in an unusually keen and precise prophetic anointing. For as long as I have known him, he has been very passionate about his relationship with the Lord and literally evangelizing the world to win the lost for Jesus Christ. In his new book, *Repairing the Broken Altar*, Apostle Hood provokes a hunger within us to find that place where God meets man and reigns down with fire. Through this timely writing, Apostle Hood offers insight and powerful truths that will grant you access to a place that God takes seriously and guards jealously. Read this book intently, and as you read it, allow it to read you. Commit yourself to God and realize that as Believers, we have an assignment and calling in the earth, through surrender and sacrifice, to repair the broken altars in our lives!

Pastor Jennifer R. Biard, Senior Pastor, Jackson Revival Center Church, Jackson, MS

REBUILDING THE BROKEN ALTAR

AWAKENING OUT OF CHAOS

GREG HOOD

Rebuilding the Broken Altar – Awakening Out of Chaos

by Greg Hood

Copyright © 2020

by Greg Hood (Global Reformation Ministries, INC)

Edit/Layout by Jim Bryson (JamesLBryson@Gmail.com)

Cover design by David Munoz (davidmunoznvtn@gmail.com)

ISBN: 978-1-7357681-0-6

Apostle Greg Hood

Global Reformation Ministries, INC

PO Box 22, Amory, MS 38821

www.greghood.org

DEDICATION

TO THE REMNANT CHURCH, THE EKKLESIA, who for the last century, have longed, prayed, fasted, sacrificed, some even giving their lives for this next great awakening.

To those who prophesied it and apostolically decreed into it.

To those who received the promise of awakening but will never see it on this side of Heaven.

May we experience it in our lifetime and pass it to the next generation who will steward it for the generation after them.

To Jesus the Christ, the King of kings and the Lord of lords, my Savior. May your Kingdom come and your will be done on earth as it is in heaven!

ACKNOWLEDGEMENTS

I WANT TO THANK MY AWESOME WIFE, JOAN, who, at the beginning of this project, prompted and encouraged me to write this book instead and put the other book on hold—the one that has been on my heart to write for some time now. Such impeccable timing. This has proven to be the right move. There is no way this book could have come about without her help and guidance through this whole process. Thank you, my Love!

A very special thanks to my editor, Jim Bryson. You came highly recommended by several of our mutual friends and you have not disappointed. Against all odds, thank you for keeping me on track and focused to get this book finished. You have taught me much.

To everyone who wrote an endorsement, proofread and gave insight for this book, I am eternally grateful. You all have impacted my life in very special ways. I am thankful for our friendships.

A big mahalo to Pastors Terry and Dori Garrett and King's Gate Worship Center in Tupelo, MS, who have allowed us to use a room as our studio from which much of this book was birthed.

Last but certainly not least by any stretch of the imagination, I want to thank my parents, Hershel and Ann Hood. From my birth, you have instilled in me to pursue my dreams and passions. You have supported me even as I have spent most of my adult life traversing the globe, preaching the gospel of the Kingdom of God, that's inherently embedded in my DNA. I am thankful for the legacy you have built within me and my brother that enables us to do what we do!

TABLE OF CONTENTS

FOREWORD

by Dutch Sheets

I HAVE ALWAYS BEEN FASCINATED by the account of Elijah and the prophets of Baal on Mount Carmel: the drama of the showdown; the efforts of the false prophets trying to conjure fire from Baal; fire from heaven falling for Elijah; and the turning of a nation back to Yahweh. What an incredible passage of scripture (see 1 Kings 18)! I have read it often, written about it, and preached from it many times, thoroughly plumbing its depths. Then, just when I thought I knew all there was to know about this passage, someone shows up and shames me! Not to mention adding insult to injury by asking me to write the Foreword.

This book is as loaded with keen insight and Spirit-inspired revelation as any you will find. You would be hard pressed to find a book more timely and more relevant for the Church and the nations—especially America—than Rebuilding the Broken Altar. Sadly, many books simply restate others' teachings, simply coloring them with a different spin. However, it is refreshing when I read a book that feeds me new thoughts and information. Simply stated, I was more than entertained and inspired by Greg's book—I learned a lot! Even though this is not just a book for pastors, I confidently say to you that you now hold a year's worth of teachings in your hand.

It had never occurred to me to apply the meanings of the 12 tribes of Israel's names to the altar Elijah built, even seeing in them what the Church needs to have restored today. And God truly is restoring them. It is so encouraging and inspiring to have someone point out the failures and weaknesses of the Church without producing hopelessness or discouragement. I finished this book with a great sense of hope for the future!

It is refreshingly clear that Greg understands and believes in America's calling and place in history, and knows it is still intact. I

1

grow weary of people stating that God is finished with America, that our sins are so grievous and many that He can't restore us. To hear them, it would seem as though America's sins are more grievous than Israel's in time past! I'm sorry to disappoint the naysayers but they are not. And thankfully, we know Israel's sins did not negate the covenant Yahweh had made with them and the purpose for which He clearly raised them up. When repentance came, purpose was restored. Similarly, the repentance that has taken place in America—which continues still—will do the same. Remember, judgment doesn't triumph over mercy; mercy triumphs over judgment (see James 2:13). Greg believes this and states his case well.

Greg also believes we win...that the Kingdom of God is an ever increasing, never ending Kingdom. No escapism. No defeatism. No evil triumphing over God and his people. He believes unequivocally that a great awakening and great harvest is coming, one of such magnitude that a billion souls will be saved and entire nations transformed. I love to read books that state the truth: God wins!

Finally, this book is refreshingly non-religious. Greg has never been known for being overly religious, something many of us find wonderfully refreshing. He keeps it real. Anyone who knows Greg knows he can be funny and true to form, the book is humorous when appropriate, without taking away from the importance of the material. You will enjoy his humor. I actually laughed out loud at times.

It is indeed my pleasure to recommend this outstanding book, *Rebuilding the Broken Altar.*

Dutch Sheets
Internationally recognized author, teacher and speaker.

Introduction

THIS BOOK HAS BEEN IN THE MAKING FOR MANY YEARS. Well, not actually pen to paper, but in my spirit. I first explored the topic of rebuilding the altar back in 1997 when I was ministering at a revival meeting in Bakersville, CA. Since then, it's been on the back burner of my mind. I would think of it from time to time, but in July of 2020, I felt to revisit it again just as a topic to minister from the pulpit to our churches. It never crossed my mind at that point to put it in print. I had another book that we were just starting to work on and hoped to finish soon. But my wife, Joan, had mentioned to me that she felt we needed to pursue this book ASAP. As we prayed into it, we both felt it timely to pursue *Rebuilding the Broken Altar*.

I had found in 1 Kings 18, a mirror of our nation's struggles and those of other nations as well. I realized, however, that if the struggle was the same, then the answer must be the same as well. We need such an encounter today in America and the world. God himself wants this.

Throughout these pages, I attempt to draw from the scripture a supernatural encounter between man and God through an altar and the fire that brings an entire nation back to God's heart.

In studying the events in 1 Kings 18, I realized that the encounter did not come without challenge. Elijah had to be willing to put everything on the line and come face to face with the real enemy of the people as he declared that God is the true God and he alone has the answers for the nation.

This message is just as true today.

God's answers are his plans, intentions and dreams for the nations and the people, and they must be accomplished in the realm of the spirit as well as the natural realm. This is not something God will do sovereignly. He will do it through his partnership with man— through you and me!

3

God has been dealing with me about the critical times that we live in, the moral and spiritual decline that our culture has reached, especially in America, and where we are headed as a nation. Any news broadcast, podcast or newspaper bears evidence of our condition. Those seeking to change our culture desire to shift America further and further away from the purpose of God for her. I believe that God is not done with America and that his plan is still to be lived out through us.

Prophetic words have been declared over America from as far back as the 17th century.

In 1607, at the first landfall at Cape Henry, the English settlers drove a wooden cross into the soil of the future great nation and dedicated the new land to the Glory of God. Robert Hunt prophesied, saying, "From these very shores the gospel shall go forth, not only to this new world, but the entire world."

In 1620, a new group of believers arrived and gave us the Mayflower compact. This was the first constitutional governing document of Plymouth Colony. Governor Bradford stated: "having undertaken for the glory of God, and advancement of the Christian faith..."

John Winthrop, a Puritan and the first governor of the State of Massachusetts, said in his 1630 writing entitled *A Model of Christian Charity*: "We shall find that the God of Israel is with us, when 10 of us shall be able to resist 1000 of our enemies, when He shall make us a praise and a glory, that men of succeeding plantations shall, 'Or we must condor that we shall be as a city upon a hill [ref Matthew 5:14], the eyes of all people upon us."

This Beatitude passage from Matthew 5:14 has been a prophetic scripture over this nation for the last 400 years.

> *Ye are the light of the world. A city set on a hill cannot be hid.*

I believe this is for our nation. Several presidents, no less than 12, believed it as well. President John F. Kennedy used the passage in a 1961 speech. President Ronald Reagan also used it in his farewell address to the nation.

> *I have spoken of a Shining City all my political life... In my mind it was a tall, proud city built on rocks stronger than oceans, windswept, God-blessed and teeming with people of all kinds living in harmony and peace; a city with free ports that hummed with commerce and creativity. And if there had to be city walls, the walls would have doors and the doors were open to anyone with the will and the heart to get there. That's how I saw it, and I still see it.*

The more Joan and I prayed the more we felt this book was a mandate from the Lord for the Church to awaken and position itself for a great awakening. This is our passion.

Now, there are things written here that could be offensive to some. We do not shy from challenging cultural and political correctness, especially within the church. I identify things that we may not be so keen to address, much less change. Culture itself can be a force for good when it upholds godly standards. This is why we must allow Holy Spirit to displace things in our cultures that do not line up with the culture of the Kingdom of God.

So, as you find things here that may challenge you culturally or politically, please don't stop reading, but press on in. I believe that Holy Spirit will begin to reshape some of your viewpoints as he has mine over the years. By no means have I arrived, but the journey has proven exciting as well as challenging as God reshapes my body, soul and spirit. You may also have some important feedback for me as well. My contact information is in the back, and I welcome your input.

Despite the present darkness of the world, there is much hope within these pages. I want to encourage you that, as you read, keep in mind that our Father is a redemptive God and that everything he does is out of his redemptive nature. He wants to restore all things and sum them up in Jesus.

We need you! The Church needs you! We need you as God has called you! In your anointing and calling, you are a vital part of the Body of Christ and this great awakening that we are on the threshold of. We will do this together—all of us and all of God.

This idea of the world getting worse and worse in order for Jesus to return has reigned in Western Christianity for decades. Thankfully, that thinking is coming to an end. AMEN! Jesus is returning for a victorious church, one without spot or wrinkle. There is winning in our future. Measurable wins! The gloom and doom of Western Christianity is on life support. Let's yank the plug. Jesus WINS!

God has given us as a nation a window of mercy to reach in and get things into alignment to be that City on a hill. He has been rearranging this nation governmentally, as well as financially so the Ekklesia (church) can reposition to bring about, by the power of Holy Spirit, the greatest awakening in the history of this planet.

This book contains Kingdom Keys that will enable us to bring about the heart and will of the Father for the earth NOW! So, while I offer a clearer glimpse into the darkness and chaos surrounding us, I also provide keys to stir up and release through you a greater light to dispel that darkness like never before; to awakening now.

As we journey through these pages together, I believe we will emerge from the final chapter with a worldview saying we don't just need change in our nations and the church, but we are that change.

 For if by the transgression of the one, death reigned through the one, much more those who receive the abundance of grace and of the gift of righteousness will reign in life through the One, Jesus Christ.

Romans 5:17

THE ALTAR

GOD IS MOVING IN THE WORLD TODAY, establishing his kingdom on earth and seeking our participation. Yet we can easily ignore, overlook or misunderstand all that God is doing.

There is a difference between God working in our midst and God working through us. We are called to partner with God—speak his words, call forth his will, declare deliverance and freedom in the earth, but we can't do that as long as we are out of step with him. We must be focused on him and not the conditions around us. On the surface, everything could be falling apart, going to hell, succumbing to sin. But on a deeper level, God is transforming our world, reclaiming it for his people. When we fail to discern what God is doing, we risk failing to do our part, even if that part is to stand fast, pray and believe.

> Of the sons of Issachar, men who understood the times, with knowledge of what Israel should do, their chiefs were two hundred; and all their kinsmen were at their command.
>
> 1 Chronicles 12:32

How do we share in what God is doing? How can we know what our part is? It starts in the core of our being, the place of surrender, honor and reverence before God. It starts at the altar—the meeting place of God and man.

We read of a similar struggle in the life of the prophet Elijah, from 1 Kings 18. Let's take this a passage at a time.

Now it happened after many days that the word of the Lord came to Elijah in the third year, saying, "Go, show yourself to Ahab, and I will send rain on the face of the earth." So Elijah went to show himself to Ahab. Now the famine was severe in Samaria.

1 Kings 18:1-3

This parallels where we are today in the United States and the world. We have, in large part, forsaken the ways of the Lord, and this has brought us to the place we find ourselves where deception and death reign through confusion, fear and lawlessness.

Thankfully, our God is a saving God. He always does things with a redemptive purpose in mind. God is not through with the nations. Indeed, the trouble we see on one level is a sign that he is working on another level. We might see the disrupted soil and question what God is doing, all the while missing the plow and the seeds of restoration being planted into fertile grounds.

No, God has not determined which nations will be goat nations and which will be sheep nations. The world is changing, evolving, growing. Nations can be turned and saved. In nations where God has given us an assignment such as Australia, the Philippines, Korea as well as the United States, God is doing great things. Understanding the message of the prophet Elijah in this particular passage is key to our ability to begin posturing and shaping the nations again.

When Ahab saw Elijah, Ahab said to him, "Is this you, you troubler of Israel?" He said, "I have not troubled Israel, but you and your father's house have, because you have forsaken the commandments of the Lord and you have followed the Baals. Now then send and gather to me all Israel at Mount Carmel, together with 450 prophets of Baal and 400 prophets of the Asherah, who eat at Jezebel's table."

1 Kings 18:17-19

In this passage, the prophet Elijah meets with Ahab, the King of Israel, and tells him that he is troubling the nation because he has forsaken the commandments and direction of God. The trouble Elijah refers to is evidenced by a crippling drought that has afflicted Israel for several years.

Ahab has followed his wife, Jezebel, and turned to Baal worship, a form of demonic paganism. Most of Israel follows Ahab's example as Jezebel endeavors to slaughter all the prophets of God. Elijah, at God's command, is ready for a showdown, so he challenges Ahab to gather all the people of Israel to Mount Carmel.

> *So Ahab sent a message among all the sons of Israel and brought the prophets together at Mount Carmel. Elijah came near to all the people and said, "How long will you hesitate between two opinions? If the Lord is God, follow Him; but if Baal, follow him." But the people did not answer him a word. Then Elijah said to the people, "I alone am left a prophet of the Lord, but Baal's prophets are 450 men. Now let them give us two oxen; and let them choose one ox for themselves and cut it up, and place it on the wood, but put no fire under it; and I will prepare the other ox and lay it on the wood, and I will not put a fire under it. Then you call on the name of your god, and I will call on the name of the Lord, and the God who answers by fire, He is God." And all the people said, "That is a good idea."*

1 Kings 18:20-24

Elijah is confident in the faithfulness of God, but note also the confidence of the prophets of Baal. They go up to Mount Carmel fully expecting to prevail. Where does such confidence come from? It comes from past experience. God is not the only source of miracles in that day. As long as the people align themselves with the powers of darkness, that power will manifest.

Just as God is doing in our nation today, in this passage, God is letting things get to the breaking point for a reason—to bring things to light.

So Elijah said to the prophets of Baal, "Choose one ox for yourselves and prepare it first for you are many, and call on the name of your god, but put no fire under it." Then they took the ox which was given them and they prepared it and called on the name of Baal from morning until noon saying, "O Baal, answer us." But there was no voice and no one answered. And they leaped about the altar which they made. It came about at noon, that Elijah mocked them and said, "Call out with a loud voice, for he is a god; either he is occupied or gone aside, or is on a journey, or perhaps he is asleep and needs to be awakened." So they cried with a loud voice and cut themselves according to their custom with swords and lances until the blood gushed out on them. When midday was past, they raved until the time of the offering of the evening sacrifice; but there was no voice, no one answered, and no one paid attention.

1 Kings 18:25-29

Notice the actions of the prophets of Baal— *they leaped about the altar which they made.* They cut themselves, offering their life-blood and proving their worthiness to their god. They do all kinds of despicable things upon that altar, but it gets them nowhere. Even the people are getting bored.

That's when Elijah steps up. He knows God will respond to his prayers, but not before he (Elijah) addresses the broken altar of God.

Then Elijah said to all the people, "Come near to me."
So all the people came near to him.

1 Kings 18:30

This is the hour that we are living in. We must say to the people of this nation and the world, "Come near to me. I have something to say; I have got something to show you."

Still, there are a lot of *words* in circulation today, a plethora of prophetic messages and teachings. Some tell us to comply with the flow of society and the edicts of governmental authorities. Others implore us to separate and withdraw from the "world systems." Each side supports their position with scripture. Most of us are caught in the middle, confused and being pulled this way and that, struggling to hear God in the din.

Like Elijah, we have to reach a place to where we hear what God is saying.

Elijah is confident that he has a word from God. Let's face it: The odds of 850 to 1 are not very good odds...unless that 1 has the infinite God on his side.

> *And he [Elijah] repaired the altar of the Lord which had been torn down. Elijah took twelve stones according to the number of the tribes of the sons of Jacob, to whom the word of the Lord had come, saying, "Israel shall be your name."*

> 1 Kings 18:30-31

Now, get this picture. Elijah has 850 frustrated and armed-to-the-teeth Baal prophets ready for him to fail so they can cut him to bits, and the first thing he does is rearrange some rocks?

Really?

Hey God, save me and your nation of Israel from these demon-fed assassins, but first, let me get these boulders in the right place.

Yeah, that's exactly what he did.

> *So with the stones he built an altar in the name of the Lord, and he made a trench around the altar, large enough to hold two measures of seed. Then he arranged the wood and cut the ox in pieces and laid it on the wood. And he said, "Fill four pitchers with water and pour it on the burnt offering and on the wood." And he said, "Do it a second time," and they did it a second time. And he said, "Do it a third time," and they did it a third time. The water flowed around the altar and he also filled the trench with water.*

> 1 Kings 18:32-35

Elijah is challenging the reigning force of evil in his day, counting on God to respond to his preparation of the sacrifice. So, after arranging the rocks into an altar, he pours water all over it, soaking the wood, the dirt, even the bull.

So, why did he use all that water, especially in the midst of a three-year drought? Three reasons.

First, it's clear that Elijah got the water from the people because earlier in the story, we see King Ahab sending people throughout the land to search for water and finding none. So, this must have been the populace's personal stash. Now, imagine the faith it takes for the people to make such a sacrifice of that precious commodity. This is about more than showing off; it's about having a dog in the hunt. The people are being asked to commit life-giving water to prove that God is the God of Israel.

Second, Elijah needed to cleanse the altar, both physically and, more importantly, spiritually. The water represented a spiritual cleansing.

> *So that He might sanctify her, having cleansed her by the washing of water with the word*

> Ephesians 5:26

Finally, the water demonstrated God's dominion over the demonic realm in the form of Baal. God had stopped the rain in Israel, and he would restore it...if the people gave their all.

They did and God did and the rest is history.

> *At the time of the offering of the evening sacrifice, Elijah the prophet came near and said, "O Lord, the God of Abraham, Isaac and Israel, today let it be known that You are God in Israel and that I am Your servant and I have done all these things at Your word. Answer me, O Lord, answer me, that this people may know that You, O Lord, are God, and that You have turned their heart back again." Then the fire of the Lord fell and consumed the*

> *burnt offering and the wood and the stones and the dust,*
> *and licked up the water that was in the trench.*
> *When all the people saw it, they fell on their faces; and*
> *they said, "The Lord, He is God; the Lord, He is God."*

1 Kings 18:36-38

God heard Elijah's prayer. The fire fell. The sacrifice was consumed. And the people were changed.

As great as this miracle was, it is too easy to focus on the spectacle of what God did and miss what it took for God to do it. Like the newly freed children of Israel who rejoiced that the Red Sea opened but later fell into worshiping a golden calf, we can miss the true process at work as God performs miracle after miracle.

Elijah's motive for following God was crucial to the successful outcome that day, just as our motives are for everything we do. If we are seeking to do anything instead of expanding the Kingdom of God and turning people's hearts to God, then we are missing the mark. Even if we are having great success, drawing people to us, exercising our gifts, seeing fire fall from heaven. If our motives are wrong, we are on the pathway to error. We cannot allow that to happen. We have to keep our hearts constantly before the Father. You know, having a shower in a house does no good if we don't step into it from time to time...preferably with nothing to hide behind.

Elijah knew that the stakes could not have been greater. The fate of God's nation hung in the balance. Evil reigned, figuratively and literally, for years. It was time to right that wrong. And yet, the first thing he did was rebuild the altar of God that had been torn apart through Baal worship.

It is time to take up our part in rebuilding the broken altar of the Lord—the place where God meets man and the fire of God falls. God does not reveal his presence just anywhere. There has to be an altar—a surrender, a sacrifice, place satisfactory to God to pour out his Holy Spirit into the earth.

The things of God are holy; they are pure; they are intimate. His Spirit is so precious that Jesus warned of unforgiveness for anyone who would commit blasphemy against it.

> *Therefore I [Jesus] say to you, any sin and blasphemy shall be forgiven people, but blasphemy against the Spirit shall not be forgiven.*

Matthew 12:31

In David's time, God killed a man who touched his ark without proper preparation.

> *But when they came to the threshing floor of Nacon, Uzzah reached out toward the ark of God and took hold of it, for the oxen nearly upset it. And the anger of the Lord burned against Uzzah, and God struck him down there for his irreverence; and he died there by the ark of God.*

2 Samuel 6:7

God even tried to kill Moses when the future deliverer of the nation failed to circumcise his son.

> *Now it came about at the lodging place on the way that the Lord met him [Moses] and sought to put him to death. Then Zipporah [Moses' wife] took a flint and cut off her son's foreskin and threw it at Moses' feet, and she said, "You are indeed a bridegroom of blood to me." So He [God] let him alone. At that time she said, "You are a bridegroom of blood"—because of the circumcision.*

Exodus 4:24-26

The power of God is serious business. We are playing with fire when we depart from pure motives. The stakes could not be greater. The fate of God's kingdom hangs in the balance.

Think about it:

If God would pour out his glory anywhere, we would have it already.

If God would pour out his glory in the biggest places, we would have it already.

If God would pour out his glory in the smallest places, we would have it already.

If God would pour out his glory in the most prosperous places or the most elegant or sophisticated places, even the most educated places, we would have it already.

If God would pour out his glory in the weirdest or flakiest places of present-day Christian mania, we would have it already.

Well, we don't have it already. Not yet, anyway.

God is intentional about where he pours out his glory. Wherever he brings his blessing, his Spirit moves in magnitudes that shift nations. He takes his Spirit seriously and guards him jealously.

REPAIR

God is giving us insight today about how to repair what has been broken. Consider the origins of the word *repair*, or *re-pair*. It implies that there was a time when the object in question was paired, right? When you pair something, you connect two things together. When you *re-pair*, you pair it again.

We pair things so they work together. People are paired in partnership, business, marriage, ministry and friendship. To be effective, the pair must share a common language. That does not mean they are identical. It means there is enough commonality to communicate, to share perspectives and resources and work toward a mutual goal.

In the history of mankind, there was a time when heaven and earth were paired. It started in the garden, but it was disrupted by Adam's disobedience. Later, God established laws for man to follow. As long as they obeyed, the pairing of heaven and earth worked reasonably well. But when man turned from the God of heaven to false gods, idols and demons, the pairing was interrupted.

Such was the case in 1 Kings 18 when the prophet Elijah repaired the altar to restore the pairing between heaven and earth.

Israel had strayed from God, but Elijah came and declared: "I am going to repair this altar so that we can encounter God again."

This endeavor continues today. God is bringing us into a place to repair the connection between heaven and earth. We do not need better preaching or more zeal or people with greater degrees to break down the word of God for us. God is ready. Earth is prime. The harvest is ripe. We must restore that synchrony between heaven and earth, as Jesus instructed us when praying.

> *Our Father who is in heaven,*
> *Hallowed be Your name.*
> *Your kingdom come.*
> *Your will be done,*
> *On earth as it is in heaven*

> Matthew 6:9-10

Notice that the request for the kingdom is followed by the implementing of God's will. *"Your kingdom come,"* and then *"Your will be done on earth as it is in heaven."* We want God's kingdom to come to earth, and we acknowledge that it will be accomplished through God's will.

There is a great awareness of the kingdom today on the earth. Some people are calling it as such; others speak of the things pertaining to the Kingdom of God but do not use that term. They talk about the need for justice, righteousness, love, peace and mercy. They are people seeking the kingdom but they don't know it yet. Why? Because we haven't demonstrated God to them. We haven't repaired the altar yet.

WITHOUT MEASURE

People are instrumental in building the Kingdom of God on earth, and they do so with the will of God at the forefront of their hearts. God meets man wherever he can, in whatever measure afforded him. As such, God is limited by the limitations of man. Repairing the altar by putting the stones in place, and by understanding what those stones represent, creates a dynamic in

16

which God moves on the earth not in a limited way but in an unmeasurable way.

This is the connection Jesus referred to in John 3:

> *He who comes from above is above all, he who is of the earth is from the earth and speaks of the earth. He who comes from heaven is above all. What He has seen and heard, of that He testifies; and no one receives His testimony. He who has received His testimony has set his seal to this, that God is true. For He whom God has sent speaks the words of God; for He gives the Spirit without measure.*

> John 3:31-34

Are you ready for this environment? Please consider this question seriously. Do you want God's Spirit *without measure*?

God says we can have the Spirit without measure, just as Jesus had it. In fact, to do all God has foretold, we must have it to that extent. But we must be ready for it. Power without preparation will kill us; it will destroy rather than establish what God desires.

Paul wrote to the Ephesians explaining that the preparation for the Spirit without measure was the reason for the five-fold ministerial gifts.

> *And He gave some as apostles, and some as prophets, and some as evangelists, and some as pastors and teachers, for the equipping of the saints for the work of service, to the building up of the body of Christ; until we all attain to the unity of the faith, and of the knowledge of the Son of God, to a mature man, to the measure of the stature which belongs to the fullness of Christ.*

> Ephesians 4:11-13

Notice that Paul did not identify crusades or book sales or conventions or kingdoms of religion as the end goal, but rather to equip us for the work of the ministry to attain the unity of faith, the knowledge of the Son of God and maturity and fullness of stature—the fullness of Christ in us

See, religion says these goals are to be accomplished in the future after the return of Jesus Christ, but Paul did not say that. Read the meaning of his words carefully. He's saying that we are to bring the body of Christ into a full measure of Christ. Religion allows us to become complacent, even lazy. "Okay. We will do what we can now. But nobody will have the full measure of Christ until we all get to heaven."

This misses God's point entirely. We are not getting into heaven. Heaven is getting into us. *"Your kingdom come"* is not the same as "Take us to your kingdom." Notice the directional arrows here.

Holy Spirit, through Paul, is telling us we attain the full measure of Christ now! Indeed, we must attain the full measure of Christ to see the fulfillment of the manifestation of the kingdom. We are not there yet. But we are getting there. Striving to attain the Spirit of God without measure is teaching us how to walk in that reality *now*. The journey qualifies us to possess the object of our quest.

After Jesus was crucified, he rose again, ascended into heaven and sat down at the right hand of the Father. From there, he sent the third person of the Trinity, Holy Spirit, to teach us and guide us.

> But the Helper, the Holy Spirit, whom the Father will send in My name, He will teach you all things, and bring to your remembrance all that I said to you.

> John 14:26

In his final days on earth with the disciples, Jesus taught primarily on the promise and role of Holy Spirit, preparing the church for the return of the governor of the kingdom back to earth.

> But when He, the Spirit of truth, comes, He will guide you into all the truth; for He will not speak on His own initiative, but whatever He hears, He will speak; and He will disclose to you what is to come. He will glorify Me,

for He will take of Mine and will disclose it to you. All things that the Father has are Mine; therefore I said that He takes of Mine and will disclose it to you.

John 16:13-15

Unfortunately, through some poor eschatology in the past, we have become satisfied with merely maintaining the religious status quo until the Lord returns, thinking that our job is to stay the course until Jesus arrives to make everything right.

Today, we know better. We are not here to tread water while waiting for the rescue boat. We are to swim to shore. Think of it. Swimmers don't get stronger by treading water, do they? Neither do Christians grow to full stature by standing still, holding ground and waiting for reinforcements.

We must dismiss these thought patterns from our lives. Yes, we must occupy until he comes, but what do we mean by *occupy*? It literally means to do business on the king's behalf. Hallelujah! We have to do business, expand the kingdom and bring an awakening of God, in God, and through God to the nations of the earth. This is the mandate we carry. We do not do it alone, but neither does God do it alone.

John Wesley put it aptly: "Without God, man cannot; without man, God will not."

THE TWELVE STONES

When Elijah repaired the altar of God, he used 12 stones. Each stone stood for one of the 12 tribes of Israel—the lineage of Jacob through his 12 sons. Each tribe possessed a unique call of God and characteristics, and from these flowed each tribe's purpose and function.

The 12 tribes (from Genesis 30) are these:

Reuben	Dan	Issachar
Simeon	Naphtali	Zebulun
Levi	Gad	Joseph
Judah	Asher	Benjamin

To understand what is required today for God's fire to fall, we must understand what each of these stones mean, what they represent and what their role is to see awakening come to America and the other nations of the world.

The Stone of Reuben

Vision

IN 1 KINGS 18, THE PROPHET ELIJAH TOOK 12 STONES from the altar that had been broken by the prophets of Baal, and he repaired them. In this context, *repair* means "to heal or cleanse," not from physical sickness but from the spiritual corruption of Baal worship. After Elijah repaired the stones, he rebuilt the altar of the Lord...with devastating consequences to the demonic prophets.

Each stone represents one of the tribes of Israel, and each tribe shows us the qualities of God that he is looking for today in a spiritual altar before his power will fall. In this chapter, we will look at the stone of Reuben to understand its integral role in the rebuilding of the altar.

Reuben was the firstborn of Jacob and Leah. The literal meaning of the name *Reuben* means "behold a son." Recall that names in the Old Testament were a prophetic vision of what that child was supposed to be. They conveyed a blessing when the person lived according to their name, and they conveyed a curse when the person failed to live according to their name.

From Reuben's name, we get: "behold the vision, to become aware, distinguished, to advise, to look, look and saw, see as a seer, to make an inspection., to understand, to provide, to belong." Let's look at some of these qualities.

BEHOLD THE VISION

The word *vision* in "behold the vision" bears closer examination. Here are three scriptures to understand *vision*.

> Now the boy Samuel was ministering to the Lord before Eli and word from the Lord was rare in those days, visions were infrequent.

1 Samuel 3:1

In this case, the King James translation gives us a better wording.

> The word of the LORD was precious in those days; there was no open vision.

1 Samuel 3:1 KJV

Vision is important for where we are going and what we are doing. However, anyone can have a vision. The distinction is that God's visions bear godly fruit. When God does things, he does them with redemption in mind.

Today, there are few open visions because we have too few apostolic and prophetic people who are willing to stick their necks out in the midst of chaos, trouble and persecution to decree God's will. Yet God is raising up his Ekklesia that would dare say, "We do not love our lives unto death. We overcome by the blood of the Lamb. We overcome by the word of our testimony and we are going to step out and we are going to begin to prophesy and we are going to begin to decree what God is telling us in our spirit to release so that the nations can be healed and God's kingdom can expand in the earth."

The second scripture is from Proverbs:

> Where there is no vision, the people are unrestrained, but happy is he who keeps the law.

Proverbs 29:18

The word *unrestrained* here means: "to let go, to let alone, loneliness, abandonment, neglect."

The same verse in the KJV reads:

> *Where there is no vision, the people perish: but he that keepeth the law, happy is he.*

Proverbs 29:18 KJV

Yet the God's Word Translation puts it best:

> *Without prophetic vision, people run wild, but blessed are those who follow [God's] teachings.*

Proverbs 29:18 GWT

Part of the definition of *vision* means "dream." God is bringing prophetic dreams back to his church. We are recapturing the imagination and valuing it. By dreams, I don't necessarily mean sleep dreams, but goals and aspirations, things so grand, so beyond our present reality that all we can do is imagine them. Yet God will bring them to pass.

Vision also means "revelation" as when God drops into our spirit things of the Spirit that we cannot understand without his intervention.

From *revelation*, we can derive the definitions: "oracle, speak, prophetic word."

Our third scripture is from 1 Timothy:

> *This command I entrust to you, Timothy, my son, in accordance with the prophecies previously made concerning you, that by them you fight the good fight,*

1 Timothy 1:18

In essence, Paul is saying: "Timothy, I want you to fight with the prophetic words spoken over you."

Prophetic words are part of the vision for our lives. They come from the heart of God. When true Prophets speak the word of the Lord over our nation, they are reading from the book concerning America.

What book? Glad you asked. From Daniel 7:10, we read:

> *The court sat, and the books were opened.*

In Psalm 139, we are told that God has all of our days numbered in a book.

> *Your eyes have seen my unformed substance;*
> *And in Your book were all written*
> *The days that were ordained for me,*
> *When as yet there was not one of them.*

Psalm 139:16

There are books about cities and nations. There are many books in heaven, not just the Book of Life. There are books that contain God's vision for each of our lives. Prophets and seers need to prophesy from these books to speak the vision of God

God is awakening fresh vision and bringing it into the church. *"Without prophetic vision people run wild."* Where there is no dream, no mental insight, no revelation, where nobody is speaking what is in the books of heaven, the people are unrestrained and running amok.

God is corralling the Ekklesia back into her place with vision, saddling and putting the bit into the mouth of the Ekklesia so he can run with us and steer us into the places he wants us to go while harnessing the power that that Ekklesia carries. We become like horses running in the battle. We must be people with vision.

What is the vision of God for your life, your spiritual house, your region, state and nation? Your personal vision will tie into the vision of the house you belong to, and the house will be ordained to bring breakthrough into the region, state, nation and the world.

No one is a Lone Ranger. The vision God gives is not for you alone; it is to serve others. The gifts are to enhance other lives, not to make you a big star. The anointing is for influence, favor, voice, impact and release of heaven's heart into what God has called you to function. *Welcome to the garden, Adam. Now get to work.*

"Happy is he who keeps the law."

The word *law* here is powerful. It means "direction." So, we could say: "Happy is he who keeps the direction."

It also means "instruction" or "to be taught." So, we could say, "Where there is no vision, the people run wild, they are unrestrained, they perish, but happy is he who stays on course, who keeps the direction, who heeds to instruction and teaching."

The word *teaching* refers to our spiritual teacher, Holy Spirit.

> *But you have an anointing from the Holy One...*
>
> 1 John 2:20

> *But when He, the Spirit of truth, comes, He will guide you into all the truth; for He will not speak on His own initiative, but whatever He hears, He will speak; and He will disclose to you what is to come.*
>
> John 16:13

So, "Happy is his who follows the instruction of Holy Spirit."

SALVATION

Hebrews 2:3 says:

> *How will we escape if we neglect so great a salvation? After it was at the first spoken through the Lord, it was confirmed to us by those who heard...*

Salvation does not mean a ticket to heaven. The word *salvation* means "to be saved, healed, delivered, set free and made whole." It is a three-step process.

- We *were* saved—past
- We *are being* saved—present
- We *will be* saved--future

Present salvation refers to the ongoing work of redeeming the body, soul and spirit. It is a recovery from the ravages of sin and the establishment of us as true sons and daughters of God.

Many people are only living the past part—salvation is an introduction to the forgiveness of God through the blood of Jesus Christ. And yet there's more, so much more.

It's time to be set free, delivered, healed and made whole. It is time to stand as adult children of the King. It is time to get to work. This is the present salvation we must not neglect.

The consequences of ignoring so great a salvation include: "to let alone, to neglect, to be out of control."

Cities in America—where murders and thieves run wild—lack godly vision. There is no direction or authority set in place to bring order so that God's heart for that city will be manifest. Parts of our society are out of control, drawn away by ignorance, influenced by powers of darkness wielding death. Poverty—both physical and spiritual—is a powerful motivator, but unless we have the true answer in hand, unless we have God's will and provision for our lives, we will react poorly to our condition and cause more damage to ourselves and our communities in the long run.

Today, regions of American are falling under the power of forces exploiting our weaknesses and spreading chaos through lies of distortion and disinformation. They purport to offer solutions but their true vision is the destruction of all God has instilled in our great country.

> *The thief comes only to steal and kill and destroy; I [Jesus] came that they may have life, and have it abundantly.*

John 10:10

GODLY VISION

Habakkuk wrote about vision and all that it entails.

> *I will stand on my guard post*
> *And station myself on the rampart;*
> *And I will keep watch to see what*
> *He will speak to me,*
> *And how I may reply when I am reproved.*
> *Then the Lord answered me and said,*
> *"Record the vision*
> *And inscribe it on tablets,*

That the one who reads it may run.
For the vision is yet for the appointed time;
It hastens toward the goal and it will not fail.
Though it tarries, wait for it;
For it will certainly come, it will not delay."

Habakkuk 2:1-4

This passage paints a picture of vision—what God is saying and how to hear it. It starts with positioning ourselves.

The name of the Lord is a strong tower;
The righteous runs into it and is safe.

Proverbs 18:10

From the tower on the city wall, we can see farther than anybody on the ground. We can see the armies that may be camped out in the field. We can the enemy approaching or a storm is coming, and we can prepare the city. When we inhabit the tower, we can see and prepare.

"I will keep watch to see what he will speak to me."

So how do we watch what somebody says? How do we watch words? We hear words; we do not watch words, right? Well, God's words are creative. He brings things into existence by his word.

God, who gives life to the dead and calls into being that
which does not exist.

Romans 4:17

Consider from Genesis 1:

God said, "Let there be light"; and there was light.
God said, "Let there be an expanse in the midst of the
waters..."
God said, "Let the waters below the heavens be
gathered into one place, and let the dry land appear..."

Got the picture? God spoke a word and the universe was created.

27

A vision from God conveys much. The word *vision* in Habakkuk means: "a dream, a sight, mental revelation, oracle, vision, to prophesy, to provide." This is why we don't have to worry about lack a of strength or resources in fulfilling our calling. When God gives us a word, it comes with it the provision we need to do what he has assigned us to do.

Anytime God gives us a vision, provision is attached to it. This is good news! God has everything we need. The elements of the world cannot stop us. Jesus calms the sea, stills the wind and rebukes the storm. Sure, we might need to press in little harder, dig a little deeper, pray harder in the Spirit, but there is provision for the vision.

"Where God guides, he provides." It's a familiar cliché but bears great truths.

How do we respond when we hear God? We inscribe it in our hearts, we pray into it and we respond with: *Yes Lord!* We respond in faith, obedience and joy. "Yes Lord here am I send me. God, I know that nothing is impossible with you."

My assistant Pastor at Life Church in Hawaii, Pastor Rick Amous, would always say he is in the "Yes Program." It's always *Yes* to God.

That is why it is important to record the word God gives us, to write it out so we keep praying about it, declaring it and remembering that we may execute it. God brings laborers for the harvest, not just for the harvest of souls but for everything that we have administered.

God wants to bring things into our lives to accomplish his vision. It takes money, energy, resources, laborers—things that we cannot get on our own. It takes others who will hear our vision and say, "I can run with this vision. I want to be a part of what God is calling you to do. Here is some money, a building, a vehicle to do this. I am praying with you, standing with you, interceding with you, that is going to be my part." That is how resources come in from many directions to fulfill the vision that God has given us.

When Reuben's stone is out of place, we experience lack of vision, perishing, running wild, hesitation and poverty.

These things hinder us from accomplishing the God-given vision and assignment in our lives. Then, not understanding the spiritual realities involved, we find ourselves fussing at God, saying "God why have you not done what you promised? Why have you not made this happen yet? This is a partnership."

I assure you, it's not God's fault. He longs to give us all these things and more.

When the altar of God is repaired (re-paired-as in "pairing" a device with Bluetooth), people will pair with you and help fulfill the assignment God has given you.

We give up too quickly. God's fulfillment comes on his schedule, but it requires our participation.

> *For the vision is yet for the appointed time;*
> *It hastens toward the goal and it will not fail.*
> *Though it tarries, wait for it;*
> *For it will certainly come, it will not delay.*

See, the word *sin* means "to miss the mark or miss the goal." In this passage, God is saying the vision is going to hit the bullseye like an arrow shot from a marksman's bow.

Sometimes, the vision is for a far-off time.

"The vision is yet for the appointed time… though it tarries…Wait for it."

What's this saying to us? Hang on; don't quit; wait for it. *"For it will certainly come, it will not delay."*

As we partner with heaven and synchronize our heart to the heart of the Father, the vision of God for our life will find that appointed time. It will manifest and expand the Kingdom of God.

Case in point: Simeon was an old man when the day finally came that he could hold the baby Jesus and bless him. Thus, his declaration:

> *Now Lord,*
> *You are releasing Your bond-servant*
> *to depart in peace,*

According to Your word;
For my eyes have seen Your salvation,
Which You have prepared in the presence of all peoples,
A Light of revelation to the Gentiles,
And the glory of Your people Israel.

Luke 2:29-32

Simeon was saying: "This is the moment I was made for." Notice that he did not change nations, part the oceans, call fire from heaven or write half the New Testament. His assignment was to bless the King. He waited his entire life...and he did it.

The bullseye you hit in your assignment makes the difference. Regardless of how it appears to the world, it will have the impact of a bomb hitting its target.

When I was 17, God said: "Greg, you will go to Australia; you will have an impact in that nation."

Well, it took me thirty-three years to get to Australia after God spoke it to me, but I never gave up. I kept pressing into the vision, believing God for provision. Many opportunities arose for me to go but I knew they were not God's time, even though I knew God said I would go.

Finally, a friend of mine, Apostle Darren Begley, said: "Hey Greg, you have shared this story several times. I want to be a part of fulfilling the vision that God gave you to go to Australia. Go with me to Australia to do a prophetic conference with some business people."

So, I did.

Although my first trip was not in a church setting as we know it. It was not in a big church service or a breakout revival. It was a conference for business people. Still, we saw the power of God manifest as we ministered and prophesied into the lives of the people. Their lives were impacted and changed. We birthed a relationship with many of those people that we hold dear still today.

It was an incredible experience, but it took me thirty-three years to get there. God's timing is perfect!

"Behold, as for the proud one, his soul is not right within him; but the righteous will live by his faith."

With a vision, we have to live by faith. We have to dream, pray, listen and hear to see these visions come to pass.

What vision has God given you? How would your life change if Reuben's stone was back in place for the fire of God to fall? What would it look like in your life today? Dream about that! Let your imagination run wild! Catch the vision that God has for you.

BEHOLD THE SON

Remember that Reuben's name means "behold the son." What does sonship mean?

Keep in mind that *son* is not gender-specific. Male and female are included in sonship. (Hey, if men can be part of the bride of Christ, women can be sons of God.)

Sonship is very important to God. The word *son* is different than the word *child.* Indeed, they are polar opposites. Let's look at the definitive passage in Galatians:

> Now I say, as long as the heir is a child, he does not differ at all from a slave although he is owner of everything, but he is under guardians and managers until the date set by the father. So also we, while we were children, were held in bondage under the elemental things of the world. But when the fullness of the time came, God sent forth His Son, born of a woman, born under the Law, so that He might redeem those who were under the Law, that we might receive the adoption as sons. Because you are sons, God has sent forth the Spirit of His Son into our hearts, crying, "Abba! Father!" Therefore you are no longer a slave, but a son; and if a son, then an heir through God. However at that time, when you did not know God, you

were slaves to those which by nature are no gods. But now that you have come to know God, or rather to be known by God, how is it that you turn back again to the weak and worthless elemental things, to which you desire to be enslaved all over again?

Galatians 4:1-9

Again, let me stress that the word *son* is not speaking of gender. The word *son* literally means "mature," as in "the mature one." In contrast, the word *child* means "immature."

The word *child* in this passage also is the Greek word for *orphan*, but the connotation is not the same as in western culture where an orphan is homeless, nameless, has no inheritance, no family. Orphan in the Bible literally means an "immature one." It is the manifestation of *child*.

In Hebrew culture, an orphan had a home, family and inheritance. He owned everything, but while he was immature (growing up), he was no different than a slave who owns nothing. He did not have possession of what was actually his. Instead, it was put under guardians until the date set by his father. Meanwhile, he was given a tutor to help raise him. This is like when we are young in Christ and Holy Spirit comes to teach and guide us (ref. John 16 and 1 John). He is our tutor.

God has put Holy Spirit in our lives to teach us to be the kings that we are. We are royalty. 1 Peter 2:9 calls us, *"a royal priesthood, a holy nation."*

Paul, in his letter to the Galatians, points out that as long as we are children, we are held in bondage by the power of the elemental things of the world. The world still has a hold on us when we are children. We love our family, our dad, our place of living, but the world keeps pulling us back, wooing us as it did to the prodigal son.

The prodigal son was an immature man who wanted something that was reserved for mature sons. It wasn't his time, but he wanted his inheritance anyway, and he got it only to waste it.

Preparation—a process which requires time—is everything. This is why, in verse 4, Paul says: *"But when the fullness of time came, God sent forth His Son born of a woman, born under the law."* That is very important. Then in verse 5: *"So that He might redeem those who were under the Law, that we might receive the adoption as sons."*

Getting the Reuben stone cleansed, healed and set in the rebuilt altar means understanding vision and sonship, and from this, walking in our identity as mature sons of God so we can transform the world.

God has a lot to say about maturity. Through the years, God has given me a few strong words about it to preach to others.

> *Tell them to get the pacifier out of their mouth and let the sword of the word of God come out of their mouths. Tell them to get out of the playpen and get on the battlefield and fight as kings fight.*

(I actually got out of those churches alive! Praise God!)

Getting the Reuben stone in place means maturing in the Lord, coming to a place where we are emerging from our selfish, bratty, "it's all about me" approach to life.

> *Because you are sons, God has sent forth the Spirit of His Son into our hearts, crying, "Abba! Father!" Therefore you are no longer a slave, but a son; and if a son, then an heir through God.*

Sometimes we know what is ours but God won't release it to us. In those instances, he's saying: "Grow up so I can release your inheritance to you. Stop living life for yourself and start living according to the vision I have given you so I can release what you know is yours for your assignment."

> *Therefore you are no longer a slave, but a son; and if a son, then an heir through God. However at that time, when you did not know God.*

Children really don't know their dads. They might know him as a provider and disciplinarian, but to know him in a way that pairs their hearts with his requires maturity. A big part of raising children is expecting them to grow up so we can have an adult to adult relationship.

Or rather to be known by God.

Interesting phrase, isn't it? We assume that God knows everybody, and in a sense, he does. But *"to be known by God"* means God is not only in our hearts, but that his heart is *synced* with ours. We are tied together for the same purposes.

> But now that you have come to know God, or rather to
> be known by God, how is it that you turn back again to
> the weak and worthless elemental things, to which you
> desire to be enslaved all over again?

As strange as this sounds, in Hebrew culture, sons grew to the appointed time when they were adopted by their fathers. Fathers adopted their sons when they saw the required maturity. This is why the word *son* not only means "mature" but also means "builder of the family name."

The adoption process was like this:

The Father calls the local leaders and businessmen to the city gate. He also invites the servants and the rest of the family. Then he stands up and says, "Today is the day that I recognize my son as one who is capable of building the family name. He is no longer a child; he is a son. I adopt him today"

He extends his arm around his son and pulls him in tight, and then in full view of everyone, he gives his son a ring, a robe and a new pair of shoes.

Yep, new shoes.

The father then declares to everyone in the city: "When you see my son coming, you see me coming. When you hear him speak, he is speaking for me because he is now a builder of the family name. We have one heart. We have one purpose. We are building this business. We are building this name together. When he asks you for something, he is not asking for himself; he is asking for me. He is a mature son. I trust him. I believe in him, and today, I make him an equal partner in the family business."

That was adoption in Hebrew culture, and it started with maturity.

Ephesians tells us:

> But God, being rich in mercy, because of His great love with which He loved us, even when we were dead in our transgressions, made us alive together with Christ (by grace you have been saved), and raised us up with Him, and seated us with Him in the heavenly places in Christ Jesus

Ephesians 2:4-6

As mature sons, we rule and reign with the Father from heavenly places. He has given us his signet ring, a robe of authority and a new pair of shoes. In so doing, he has brought us into a place as builders of the family name and partners of the business.

What is our Father's business? He is not a cobbler, carpenter, engineer or preacher. Our Father is a King. Therefore, our family business is kingdom. When God pulls you in and gives you your inheritance, he is declaring to the world: "When you see my son, you see me."

This typifies Jesus' relationship with the Father. He desires the same for us (Matthew 11:27). This is why scripture tells us:

> Where two or three have gathered together in My name, I am there in their midst.

Matthew 18:20

CONCLUSION

When the world sees mature sons and daughters of God, they see God himself. It is an identity that conveys certain privileges:

Therefore I say to you, all things for which you pray and ask, believe that you have received them, and they will be granted you.

Mark 11:2

As great as this is, *asking* of the Father does not adequately convey the intent here. Think of it as: "When you are speaking, decreeing, prophesying and expanding, you are building the family name, God is with you."

As a mature son of God, David was distinguished from his brothers. Today, as mature sons and daughters of God, we will stand out of the crowd in a purposeful way. God wants to distinguish us from our people. He wants them to see his favor on our lives. He wants to draw others to him through us.

When the Reuben stone is in place, the favor of the Lord is released on our lives. Recall that the name *Reuben* includes: "to advise." The Bible tells us that Holy Spirit advises us but also, there is wisdom in a multitude of counsel. As mature sons and daughters of God, you may be that counsel. People may reach out to you saying: "I am going through something. I have a decision to make. What do you think I should do? Could you advise me? What is it that God would say?"

When Reuben's stone is in place, you will see as a seer. You will inspect and hold accountable those things that you set in order. There will be understanding provisioned for you. You will belong to a deeper spiritual order. You will not be a wanderer or an orphan any longer.

So, what is it that happens when the Reuben stone is out of place? It's not pleasant. Reverse all of the good things. You are: "not favored, a scoundrel, a slave, doomed, the unfortunate, in a place of gloating and pride, a wanderer, an outcast, without vision, without prophetic insight, without understanding, hidden with no access, without access to the Father, unaware of purpose, unable to see your vision, unable to advise others in theirs."

I told you it wasn't pleasant.

What does it mean when Reuben's stone is in place? It means we have full access to the throne of the Father. We have prophetic insight to prophesy the will and heart of the Father. We are led by Holy Spirit, according to Romans 8:14.

> *For all who are being led by the Spirit of God, these are sons of God.*

There is understanding and revelation like we see in Ephesians 1. There is wisdom to act in the family name—the King's name. We act on behalf of the Father.

> *Therefore Jesus answered and was saying to them, "Truly, truly, I say to you, the Son can do nothing of Himself, unless it is something He sees the Father doing; for whatever the Father does, these things the Son also does in like manner.*

> John 5:19

When the Reuben stone is in place, we act on God's behalf to carry out his plans and purposes in the earth. We understand the way of the Father and have increased vision and provision for the future. Reuben's stone in place creates partnership with heaven as one who is firstborn.

> *No longer do I [Jesus] call you slaves, for the slave does not know what his master is doing; but I have called you friends, for all things that I have heard from My Father I have made known to you.*

> John 15:15

THE STONE OF SIMEON

Listening

IN BIBLE DAYS, PARENTS NAMED THEIR CHILDREN prophetically according to their destiny, declaring both what they were and what they would become. As with all things prophetic, however, if the children did not live out their destiny, the opposite of these qualities would manifest. As the leading prophet of Israel, Elijah putting the stones back into place reversed the corruption that had perverted the 12 tribes for generations, thereby restoring the purpose and call of each tribe to the nation.

What does Simeon's name signify? What characteristics does it call forth? In the Hebrew, it is *Shama* or *Shimon* and it literally means: "to announce, to completely comprehend, to diligently discern, to hear for certain, to keep on listening, to be attentive, to listen carefully, to obey."

That's a lot, right? Why do we need this in the altar of God? What is God looking for before his fire will fall?

Well, consider how many of us hear things but do not comprehend them? To comprehend requires that we listen carefully. It starts with a proclamation and it ends with being obedient to whatever we hear. If we fail to listen carefully, we either ignore what is being proclaimed or we attempt to follow it foolishly without understanding, lacking maturity like a new convert armed with a Bible verse and seeking to admonish elders.

Simeon's name also means "listen to this, overheard as listening by permission." It's like eavesdropping but it is more. It implies being given permission to listen in on a conversation, not just eavesdropping or overhearing but to be purposefully brought in to hear the intent and depth of someone's heart.

Think of being invited to the Oval Office and listening as the President discussed matters of state with the Cabinet. Most people would be honored to be there and would have the good sense to sit, be quiet and listen intently.

Today, we are encountering a generation of outspoken people with a false sense of confidence and a self-directed moral compass. These are people who have nothing of value to say but they open their mouths anyway...loudly...blatantly...forcefully...to anyone foolish enough to listen to them. This is what happens when Simeon's stone is out of place.

In contrast, when Simeon's stone is re-paired and in place, we see a generation of people who carefully obey, who are quick to listen and slow to speak.

> *This you know, my beloved brethren. But everyone must
> be quick to hear, slow to speak and slow to anger.*

James 1:19

When Simeon's stone is out of place, it means: "death with no ability to hear, ignorance with no desire to learn the truth, confusion about what is going on around us, poor spiritual stewardship, neglect of the spiritual gifts and the responsibilities given by the Father, to hear something but to be unsure of what we heard."

DEATH WITHOUT HEARING

As I have grown older, I can hear sound but cannot always discern what I am hearing unless I pay close attention to the words and the speaker. This is what it means to hear something but to be unsure of what we heard. It means "hesitation, rebellion against Father's mandate and assignment for our lives, to tune out Holy

Spirit, eavesdropping but with a distorted purpose, that we may pervert the truth and bend it to our purposes."

This describes a large portion of the church today. The church is often deaf with no ability to hear what Father is saying.

This, I believe, is because:

- We make education more important than intimacy.
- We make degrees more important than relationship with God.
- We bestow prestige on titles rather than the ability to follow after the heart of God.
- We fail to let the fruit—the results of ministry—give the title.

Today, as we grapple with titles, we are caught between competing solutions to the same malady. We either strive for titles to gain prestige or we eliminate all titles to remove the temptation to strive in vain. Either solution only furthers the problem. We don't know what to value nor how to value it.

True results are seen by the Father in secret, and it is he who rewards openly.

> But you, when you pray, go into your inner room, close
> your door and pray to your Father who is in secret, and
> your Father who sees what is done in secret will reward
> you.

Matthew 6:6

IGNORANCE IS MISS

When Simeon's stone is out of place, the church puts more importance on natural achievements than spiritual engagement and relationship with Jesus.

The opposite of the Simenon stone literally means "no ability to hear." Simply put: *ignorance*.

Consider Paul's words to the Corinthians as he taught them about the gifts of Holy Spirit:

Now concerning spiritual gifts, brethren, I do not want you to be ignorant:

1 Corinthians 12:1 NKJV

When Simeon's stone is out of place, ignorance rules.

Now, ignorance is not as bad as stupid. Like the great philosopher, Forrest Gump says: "Stupid is as stupid does." Stupid cannot be fixed. Ignorance can...sometimes. Ignorance means "unlearned without knowledge." So, there's hope. Still, there is a point when ignorance turns into stupidity. When we do not *want* knowledge and we refuse to learn, ignorance descends to another level.

As the church, we often find ourselves at a place where we do not want to learn. We do not want to know about:

- the gifts of the Holy Spirit
- the fivefold ministry
- how to judge the gifts
- how to position the gifts

For example, in 1 Corinthians 12:28, we find that God placed a specific order of government in the church.

And God has appointed in the church, first apostles, second prophets, third teachers, then miracles, then gifts of healings, helps, administrations, various kinds of tongues.

To see the power of God come, we must understand and follow God's protocol. God put it there for a reason! We cannot be ignorant about this. We cannot say, "Well, apostles no longer exist or there are so many fake apostles and prophets out there so this is not for us." Look, there's always one bad apple in the bunch. There was a Judas among the disciples, and Jesus saw him every day! Just because there are bad ones out there does not mean the God-appointed ones do not exist anymore. Focus on the order God instituted. He operates in proper order (ref. 1 Corinthians 14:33), not in great ideas or solutions just because they look and sound glamorous and are "friendly" and do not offend anybody.

No, we have to learn and be led by Holy Spirit.

> *As for you, the anointing which you received from Him abides in you, and you have no need for anyone to teach you; but as His anointing teaches you about all things, and is true and is not a lie, and just as it has taught you, you abide in Him.*

> 1 John 2:27

We must lay aside our religious traditions that are preventing the Word of God from working in our lives. We must follow Jesus' example in John 5:19 and say "Father, I am only gonna do or say what you want me to do or say and only go where you want me to go. I am not reverting to my religion or my traditions. Strip me of those things in my life. Remove anything hindering me from following you with all of my heart, and let's get Simeon's stone back in place. Let us not be ignorant concerning the things of the Kingdom of God."

Ignorance needs to be replaced with knowledge, understanding and revelation. Are you ready for that?

The Bible speaks of two kingdoms—the kingdom of darkness and the kingdom of light. The word *darkness* means "ignorance." The word *light* means "knowledge."

In Ephesians 4, notice what knowledge God values:

> *Until we all attain to the unity of the faith, and of <u>the knowledge of the Son of God,</u> to a mature man, to the measure of the stature which belongs to the fullness of Christ.*

> Ephesians 4:13 [emphasis added]

The knowledge we are seeking is that of Christ. The distinction between the kingdom of darkness and the kingdom of light is not one of good and evil. Rather, it is of ignorance and knowledge. That is why we overcome darkness by knowing Christ, and through Christ, we encounter the power of Almighty God.

When Paul was shipwrecked on a remote island, he was bitten by a viper while gathering firewood. The natives expected him to die. But instead, something else happened:

> But they were expecting that he was about to swell up or suddenly fall down dead. But after they had waited a long time and had seen nothing unusual happen to him, they changed their minds and began to say that he was a god.

Acts 28:6 [emphasis added]

The natives went from *ignorance* of God to *knowledge* of God when confronted with the *power* of God. *"They changed their minds."*

When the Simeon stone is out of place, ignorance runs rampant and the fire of God does not fall. Ignorance has reigned in the church for too long. It is time for mature sons and daughters to rise up, step into our purpose and destiny and receive our inheritance to accomplish the assignment that God has given us for his purpose. We are at the door and crossing the threshold.

CONFUSION

When the Simeon stone is out of place, we become confused with everything that is going on around us. I see this in the church today and in the world at large. The mass media controls the narrative and feeds us what they want us to hear. Without an ear toward heaven, we become a people most confused. The media does not convey truth. Rather, it conveys a sense of being well-informed. These are polar opposites.

There is confusion in the world and there is confusion in the church. Yet we are called to be the salt of the earth. We are called to be the leaders. We will inhabit the city of God someday while the nations come to us for healing.

Then he showed me a river of the water of life, clear as crystal, coming from the throne of God and of the Lamb, in the middle of its street. On either side of the river was the tree of life, bearing twelve kinds of fruit, yielding its fruit every month; and the leaves of the tree were for the healing of the nations.

Revelation 22:1-2

Just as Elijah did on that fateful day in Israel's history, we must repair Simeon's stone in the altar so we can know what God is saying and stand in the will of God, the purpose of God, and execute his instructions accordingly.

God is calling us to rise above the confusion that's infesting the earth today. We must shut some things out of our lives. We must regulate the ear-gate of our bodies, souls and spirits because what we admit determines our direction and actions. We may have to tune out CNN and tune in CN—*Christ Network*.

We are supposed to comply with the government. Yes, but only if it does not interfere with what God is doing on the earth. We must be able to look beyond the surface and see the root of things. God is bringing us into a place where we will not be confused. We will know what to do and be at peace with it.

There is an agenda of darkness to turn people into sheep. God wants us to rise up as lions and roar. Hallelujah. The enemy wants to turn our roar into a feeble *baahh*. God is calling the church to rise up with the Lion of Judah and roar, causing our enemies to shake in their boots and bow to the name of Jesus Christ.

POOR STEWARDSHIP

When Simeon's stone is out of place, it results in poor stewardship, neglecting the gifts and responsibilities given by Holy Spirit.

The chaos of the world does not relieve us of our responsibility toward God and his purposes. We cannot simply stop. We are still sons and daughters of the King. Indeed, our efforts must continue and they must intensify. God is looking for a people who are not afraid to be intense with the right motives and the right hearts in times of crisis.

Someone must defy the spirits of darkness. It is not viruses or plagues or the media or corrupt politics or popular lies that we are fighting. It is the spirit of darkness at the heart of all of these things.

God is looking for a people who will rise up as Simeon stones. As the stone is restored and the altar repaired, so will come the awakening, the revival and the outpouring of God that is in his heart to bestow. Power will flow into the earth and we will see nations shift in a single day.

For this to happen, we must hear God. We must have our theology right. We must have our relationships right. We must have our interpretation of God's word right.

How can we do this?

By tuning in to what the Father is saying and not listening to the opinions of man. Whether it is the news media or some religious rooster crowing in the pulpit, it does not matter. If they are not giving you the heart of the Father, put your ear to the chest of the Father so that you can catch his heartbeat and know what he is saying. Although you have two ears, you can only heed one source.

HESITANCY

When the Simeon stone is out of place, there is hesitancy.

There is a lot of hesitation in the church today, not just individuals debating whether or not to give a word, but people struggling to do all that God has called them to do.

Now, please do not confuse boldness with things that would be blatantly offensive to others. When we are bold in God and we step out and do what God's told us to do, there are results that God already has in mind when he put that spirit of boldness in us. We cannot fear boldness and still be effective for God. We cannot hesitate in what God has called us to do. Exercising our gifts, living

46

our assignments and coming together as the Ekklesia are all part of assembling together and all require boldness.

> *Not forsaking our own assembling together, as is the habit of some, but encouraging one another; and all the more as you see the day drawing near.*

Hebrews 10:25

I meet many Christians today who are afraid to come together. Why? Fear of persecution or disease or public perception. God is looking for that apostolic Ekklesia to step up and walk in what he has given us: power over serpents, over sickness, over hostile governments and mob rule.

We must stand to become the Ekklesia—the apostolic and prophetic people whom God has called us to be today. As such, we are going to *speak* change into the earth. We are going to *release* change in the nations. We are going to *be* the change agents in our communities and the world systems.

Delayed obedience is disobedience. We cannot hesitate.

REBELLION

When Simeon's stone is out of place, it results in rebellion against the Father's mandate and assignment for our lives. If we are out of joint with God, not following the heart of God, he is not obligated to pour out his Spirit in our lives. Indeed, he will still love us, but we are useless to his greater aims.

We quench rebellion by following the mandate and assignment of God for our lives. And we do this by tuning in to Holy Spirit.

> *For all who are being led by the Spirit of God, these are sons of God.*

Romans 8:14

If we are sons and daughters of God, we *must* be led by the Spirit of God!

Jesus said that when Holy Spirit comes, he will lead us and guide us into all truth. He will establish us in repentance, righteousness and judgment. Why? Because Holy Spirit's assignment is to fashion us into who God created us to be so that the kingdoms of this world become the kingdoms of our God.

We must stop rejecting and tuning out Holy Spirit. There are entire denominations today that refuse to acknowledge Holy Spirit. There are "moves of God" that have nothing to do with Holy Spirit. They teach that his gifts are not for today. They say healings, miracles and signs and wonders are not for today. People have turned to doubt rather than Holy Spirit. To see the fire of God fall, we must give Holy Spirit free reign in our lives.

We are to be mature sons and daughters. We cannot be moved simply by our emotion; we must be led by Holy Spirit.

CONCLUSION

When Simeon's stone is out of place, it means to eavesdrop to distort truth. Some people like to eavesdrop just so they can gossip about other people's stuff. Gossip is always a distortion of truth. (So is the media, most of the time.)

In our assignments today, we must have correct doctrine, speaking things that are theologically sound. In this endeavor, we have much to unlearn, and we can only do this by listening to God.

When I was 17 years old, Holy Spirit said, "Greg, you need to be willing to unlearn almost as much as you've you learned."

That surprised me. I thought I had been taught correctly about everything. In obedience, I had to be willing to unlearn. This was not easy for me, at least not at first.

We must be willing to address the hard things if we are going to see the fire of God fall. For the power of God to fall and the nations to be shifted in alignment with God's assignment, we must be willing to allow Holy Spirit to address things that we consider sacred to ourselves. Get ready for the slaughter of some sacred cows.

Theologians are human, just like everyone else. They are right in some things, wrong in other things, and confused more than they'd like to admit. That is why it is incumbent upon every believer to study the Word of God themselves with the prayer: "Holy Spirit teach me."

When we stop resisting Holy Spirit and start desiring truth, being willing to change things that need to change, we will see the change we desire both within us and around us.

God has trusted us, ordained us, anointed us and equipped us to hear his voice in the middle of a chaotic earth. The answer to this chaotic mess and turmoil is within us—Holy Spirit. The enemy is losing ground, losing his stronghold. It is being taken by the Kingdom of God. The Ekklesia is arising. We are becoming a piercing voice of clarity and direction. The Bible says that loud praise pierces the ear of the enemy. God wants us to be that piercing voice of clarity and direction.

> *Praise Him with loud cymbals;*
> *Praise Him with resounding cymbals.*

> Psalm 150:5

How long will we hesitate between two opinions?

If the Lord is God, serve him. If Baal is God, serve him. But do not hesitate. I decree to you that Baal is not God. It is literally the spirit of Baal that has been released in the nations today that is causing all of this crisis, all of this uproar, all of this trauma.

Yet the Spirit of God trumps everything else! God is God and no one else comes close. Let us be people who pursue knowledge and eager to learn; people who carefully listen and aptly obey that we may see the fire fall over America and the nations of the earth today. In Jesus' name!

THE STONE OF LEVI

Priesthood

FROM 1 KINGS 18, WHEN ELIJAH CHALLENGED the prophets of Baal and Asherah, we see that he first drew all of Israel to him.

> *Then Elijah said to all the people, "Come near to me." So all the people came near to him. And he repaired the altar of the Lord which had been torn down.*

1 Kings 18:30

Then, with the people around him, Elijah drew near to God.

> *At the time of the offering of the evening sacrifice, Elijah the prophet came near and said, "O Lord, the God of Abraham, Isaac and Israel, today let it be known that You are God in Israel and that I am Your servant and I have done all these things at Your word. ³⁷Answer me, O Lord, answer me, that this people may know that You, O Lord, are God, and that You have turned their heart back again."*

1 Kings 18:36-38

Thus, he joined Israel and God together, and the power of God fell in fire.

From James 4:8, we know: "*Draw near to God and He will draw near to you.*" The entirety of what we do as fivefold ministers is to guide people into a strong relationship with God, equipping them for the work of the ministry, developing a unity of the faith and maturing the Church to bring us into that fullness of Christ. This is also what the tribe of Levi was designated to do.

PRIESTS

Levi was an unusual tribe. The word *Levi* means "attached, joined to." It is from another Hebrew word meaning "to join, to be joined." It means "to attend," not in the sense of attending a football game, but rather: "to attend to something God has," as in "to join oneself, to be joined to, tied together."

Picture Levi's tribe tied to God, arm to arm, leg to leg, walking with God. They were joined to God for service. From their proximity to the Lord, they could catch the rhythm of God's heart and carrying out his intentions.

The tribe of Levi, unlike the other tribes, was given to God "to stand in place." They were the priests and they stood in the Holy of Holies—the inner sanctum of the temple, a place no one else could go into. They did not stand *before* God, however, but *with* God. This is why they are defined as "to join as one, set aside." They were set aside by God to partner with him for service.

Levi is known as the tribe of the priesthood, and they included leaders such as Moses, Aaron, Zacharias, John the Baptist and Barnabas. The tribe was designated as priests from the time when Moses called them out on Mount Sinai.

> *Now when Moses saw that the people were out of control—for Aaron had let them get out of control to be a derision among their enemies—then Moses stood in the gate of the camp, and said, "Whoever is for the Lord, come to me!" And all the sons of Levi gathered together to him.*

> Exodus 32: 25-26

Sounds like the same call that Elijah made, doesn't it? Stand for the Lord or don't stand for the Lord at all. Levi stood for God, and from that moment, they assumed their place as ministers of the tabernacle and later, the temple. Moses gives us a brief summary of their significance in his blessing over the tribe of Levi.

> *Who said of his father and his mother,*
> *"I did not consider them";*
> *And he did not acknowledge his brothers,*
> *Nor did he regard his own sons,*
> *For they observed Your word,*
> *And kept Your covenant.*
> *"They shall teach Your ordinances to Jacob,*
> *And Your law to Israel.*
> *They shall put incense before You,*
> *And whole burnt offerings on Your altar.*
> *"O Lord, bless his substance,*
> *And accept the work of his hands;*
> *Shatter the loins of those who rise up against him,*
> *And those who hate him, so that they will not rise again."*

Deuteronomy 33:9-11

The tribe of Levi was loyal to the Lord and they were assigned to teach the people of God. It goes on to say that those who rise up against Levi would be ill-advised to do so, for God was protecting them and would avenge them.

Because of their unique position with God and Israel, Levi had no tribal territory. Every other tribe got land, but the Lord was Levi's inheritance. This was by God's direction to Aaron as the head of Levi.

> *All the offerings of the holy gifts, which the sons of Israel offer to the Lord, I have given to you and your sons and your daughters with you, as a perpetual allotment. It is an everlasting covenant of salt before the Lord to you and your descendants with you." Then the Lord said to Aaron, "You shall have no inheritance in their land nor own any portion among them; I am your portion and your inheritance among the sons of Israel.*

Numbers 18:19-20

God made it clear, as he separated Levi from the rest of Israel, that he was going to be their portion and inheritance. In truth, Levi got the better deal. Later, they did receive pastureland for their cattle and some cities for their dwelling.

A NEW WINE

The duties that Levi had to adhere to were extensive. The book of Leviticus goes into great detail of their duties including rituals and sacrifices, a significant part of the law of Moses. The tribe was known throughout history as the caretakers of the tabernacle and later, the temple. However, there was eventually a shift into another type of priesthood. When Jesus ascended to heaven, he ushered in an entirely different order of priests.

For this reason, it is more accurate to understand the stone of Levi as the stone of the priesthood. God's priesthood started with the Levitical priests, but it was supplanted by Jesus Christ. So, in essence, when the stone of Levi is out of place, it means that the stone of the priesthood is missing or it's operating from a religious pattern. Today, we seek not to replace the Levitical stone but the priesthood stone.

The Levitical priesthood focused on rituals, ordinances, rules and regulations they had to follow to relate to God. Through prescribed animal sacrifices, the people's sins would be atoned for until the next year. The Levitical priests stood between God and man for centuries until Jesus, as high priest, could assume his place in the kingdom.

Although the religious order of Levi's' day knew a messiah was coming, they expected him to come in the fashion of the Levitical priesthood. And that, in part, is why they completely missed him. Jesus did not come as our high priest through the Levitical order. He came through the order of Melchizedek, and this threatened...everything (not that the Levites were even aware of it).

You see, over the centuries, the priesthood of Levi became an established, dominant force over the people, to the extent of determining whether someone would live or die. Unfortunately, with absolute power comes absolute corruption. The priesthood was not completely corrupt—good people would arise from time to time, like Zacharias (John the Baptist's father)—but it was close. As the caretakers of the relationship between God and man, the priests became complacent, opportunistic, greedy and entrenched. This is why Jesus clashed so severely with them.

As a matter of fact, every time this priest Jesus found himself in a temple, he caused trouble.

> *The Passover of the Jews was near, and Jesus went up to Jerusalem. And He found in the temple those who were selling oxen and sheep and doves, and the money changers seated at their tables. And He made a scourge of cords, and drove them all out of the temple, with the sheep and the oxen; and He poured out the coins of the money changers and overturned their tables; and to those who were selling the doves He said, "Take these things away; stop making My Father's house a place of business."*

John 2:13-16

> *It is written, "My house shall be called a house of prayer"; but you are making it a robbers' den.*

Matthew 21:13

> *Woe to you, scribes and Pharisees, hypocrites! For you clean the outside of the cup and of the dish, but inside they are full of robbery and self-indulgence.*

Matthew 23:25

Not a good idea to disrupt the livelihood of powerful people and humiliate them publicly, especially people well-connected with the most ruthless government on earth—the Roman empire.

Still, I don't think Jesus cared. In fact, he was doing exactly what he was sent to do—destroy the old priestly order and establish a new one in his name and through his life.

Jesus had calmer words for the common people and those trying to follow God through the law. When the disciples of John the Baptist asked Jesus why his disciples didn't fast as they did, he answered more than their immediate query.

> *And Jesus said to them, "The attendants of the bridegroom cannot mourn as long as the bridegroom is with them, can they? But the days will come when the bridegroom is taken away from them, and then they will fast. But no one puts a patch of unshrunk cloth on an old garment; for the patch pulls away from the garment, and a worse tear results. Nor do people put new wine into old wineskins; otherwise the wineskins burst, and the wine pours out and the wineskins are ruined; but they put new wine into fresh wineskins, and both are preserved."*

Matthew 9:15-17

Jesus was saying: "I am not coming to put new wine into an old wineskin. It would break. I did not come to fix your old broken, dilapidated religion. I came to destroy it and replace it with something entirely new—something alive and eternal."

As if that wasn't enough, Jesus foretold the destruction of the crowning jewel of Jewish life—the spectacular temple that Herod the Great built.

> *Jesus came out from the temple and was going away when His disciples came up to point out the temple buildings to Him. And He said to them, "Do you not see all these things? Truly I say to you, not one stone here will be left upon another, which will not be torn down."*

Matthew 24:1-2

Not one stone would be left over another. You would not even be able to tell that a temple was ever there. Yet he was talking total destruction of the religious order, not just a building.

56

It was when Jesus aligned his physical body with the temple, however, that he became the most divisive.

"Destroy this temple, and in three days I will raise it up."

John 2:19

Of course, he was speaking of the resurrection.

Or do you not know that your body is a temple of the Holy Spirit who is in you, whom you have from God, and that you are not your own?

1 Corinthians 6:19

Many churches today are happy with the old ways. I hear people saying all the time, "Give me some of that old-time religion." No, thank you. I want what Jesus is doing today. I want this new and living way that Jesus has brought to the earth called the Kingdom of God. It is not a religion; it is not full of ordinances and rituals. It is the rule and reign of Jesus the King, through his sons and daughters, the family of God moving together as one body, expanding the kingdom here on earth. I want this new wine that Jesus is pouring out. What about you?

Jesus not only spoke of this new wine, he demonstrated it by turning water into wine at a wedding in Cana. He was reluctant to do so at first, but he gave in to his mother's request.

When the wine ran out, the mother of Jesus said to Him, "They have no wine." And Jesus said to her, "Woman, what does that have to do with us? My hour has not yet come."
His mother said to the servants, "Whatever He says to you, do it."

John 2:3-5

Jesus pleaded with his mother that it was not his time, but he operated outside of his time because his time was only inside of him. Jesus was saying, "It is not yet the season for manifestation of who I am, but because of who I am, I can bring some of me into this."

Now, it was the third day of the wedding and the party was going strong when Jesus performed this miracle. The bridegroom, not knowing what Jesus did, tasted the wine and pronounced:

> *"Every man serves the good wine first, and when the people have drunk freely, then he serves the poorer wine; but you have kept the good wine until now."*

John 2:10

You see, Jesus did not give them the same old stuff they were drinking. He gave them something better, something symbolic of what he was bringing into the earth, something intoxicating.

Scripture often refers to Holy Spirit as wine because the Holy Spirit is intoxicating. What does it mean to be intoxicating? It means operating out of your normal state of mind. Intoxication alters everything about you—how you think, walk, speak and spend your money.

Jesus gave us new wine and a new and living priesthood through Holy Spirit in our lives. It was not just for an infilling to speak in tongues or heal the sick. It was to bring about a priestly order to the earth that has been absent since Adam—the Melchizedek priesthood. We must get this priesthood activated for the fire of God fall.

Let us look closer at the priesthood that Jesus established.

> *For it is evident that our Lord was descended from Judah, a tribe with reference to which Moses spoke nothing concerning priests. And this is clearer still, if another priest arises according to the likeness of Melchizedek, who has become such not on the basis of a law of physical requirement, but according to the power of an indestructible life. For it is attested of Him,*

"You are a priest forever According to the order of Melchizedek."
For, on the one hand, there is a setting aside of a former commandment because of its weakness and uselessness (for the Law made nothing perfect), and on the other hand there is a bringing in of a better hope, through which we draw near to God.

Hebrews 7:14-19

Jesus is the high priest, not after the Levitical priesthood but after the order of Melchizedek. These are totally different types of priesthood. Thank God Jesus was born in Judah and not in Levi. But Jesus brings another quality that the Levitical priests did not have—eternal life.

The former priests, on the one hand, existed in greater numbers because they were prevented by death from continuing, but Jesus, on the other hand, because He continues forever, holds His priesthood permanently. Therefore He is able also to save forever those who draw near to God through Him, since He always lives to make intercession for them.

Hebrews 7:23-25

"To save forever...He always lives..." Jesus functions from the power of an endless life and so should we. Hallelujah!

Getting the Levi stone back in place is installing the priest stone—a new living way, a new order. Jesus replaced Levi with Melchizedek. The kingdom operation of the priesthood is no longer under Levi's order. It is under the power of an endless life through Jesus Christ our Lord, and we are a part of Jesus' priesthood after the order of Melchizedek.

WHY PRIESTS TODAY?

When we hear the word *priest*, we might think of the Catholic or Episcopal church. Or maybe we think of the equivalent to a pastor in a Protestant denomination, someone in the pulpit on Sunday morning bringing the word. Or maybe visiting the sick, conducting weddings and funerals, baptizing people and teaching on Wednesday nights.

Such is the old order.

In the new order, the job of priests is to get things legally in place so that we can step into our kingly anointing and make decrees. As the Bible tells us in 1 Peter 2:5:

> You also, as living stones, are being built up as a spiritual house for a holy priesthood, to offer up spiritual sacrifices acceptable to God through Jesus Christ.

As priests, it is our job to get things legally in order so we can step into our kingship and make apostolic decrees. We are a royal priesthood, a kingly priesthood. Royalty speaks of kingship. Priests intercede and kings decree. Yet we cannot step into the kingly anointing without understanding the priestly anointing that God gives us in our lives through Jesus Christ. That is what we do when we intercede, we are getting things legally in alignment in our lives, establishing his glory and dominion forever.

This is not a religious function. This is a kingdom function.

- Religion wants ordinances.
- Religion wants the rituals of Levi.
- Religion wants to go through the steps so that maybe we can please God someday.
- Religion wants rituals on Sunday morning—singing, standing, kneeling, praying, hearing yet leaving the same way we came.
- Religion wants us in a holding pattern, waiting for the power of God to change things when we have already had the power working in us and through us.

This new order of priesthood is powerful because it is not religious. In this new priesthood, we are all kings and priests under the Melchizedek order through Jesus Christ. No matter if we are business people, teachers, government officials, stay at home parents, artists or entertainers...whatever sphere of society we inhabit, we carry a priestly and a kingly anointing to establish the glory and dominion of the Kingdom of God. This is how God is getting kingdom done.

The word glory is kabod in the Hebrew. It means "weight." We are to bring the weight of God in every situation we enter. The weight of God goes everywhere with us.

Now, the glory is not those chill bumps (or as we say in Hawaii, "chicken skin") that make some folks fall out in the spirit. The glory is the weight of God, the influence of God, the intimidation of God that turns the enemy away from people and situations and brings people into the kingdom. We carry the glory as born-again believers. The glory is brought by the priest. The dominion is brought by kings. Through God's dominion, we call for the kingdoms of this world to become the kingdoms of our God. He has given us power and authority over the enemy, and nothing shall harm us.

> *Behold, I have given you authority to tread on serpents and scorpions, and over all the power of the enemy, and nothing will injure you.*

Luke 10:19

As kings and priests, we apply that scripture to wherever we find the enemy working. In abortion, government, schools, the economy, through greed, oppression and deception. Transsexuals and transvestites are indoctrinating our young children, reading stories to them that support their lifestyle. I read of a stripper instructing a third-grade class on how to pole dance. This is not spiritual warfare in the ether somewhere. This is wickedness right under our noses. It is happening in our homes and communities. If you don't believe me, check your kid's internet usage and monitor what's being taught at their school.

As bad as this sounds, however, here is the good news. We have the power to overcome it.

God is looking for sons and daughters who will rise up and say, "I will be that priest and that king in the business realm, government realm, arts and entertainment realm, media realm, family realm, ministry realm and educational realm. I will be the voice of reason, the voice of God and his kingdom to proclaim his goodness, bring his glory and establish his dominion in this place."

The religious priesthood would not do this. A Sunday morning pastor does not do this. A professional minister cannot ever do this. It has to be Spirit-grown sons and daughters coming to a place where we understand our position, power and responsibilities. It's a matter of getting the stone of the priesthood into place through Jesus Christ.

> *Have made us kings and priests to our God,*
> *And we shall reign on the earth.*
>
> Revelation 5:10 NKJV

This is not a post-millennial event; this is a now event. This is not scheduled for the future. This is not the end times foretold by Revelation. This is now.

> *For if by the transgression of the one, death reigned through the one, much more those who receive the abundance of grace and of the gift of righteousness will* <u>*reign*</u> *in life through the One, Jesus Christ.*
>
> Romans 5:17 [emphasis added]

The word *reign* literally means "to become king." God has put a kingly and priestly anointing on us to release God's glory and dominion.

Wherever He has given you authority, whatever sphere of influence that he has put you in, it is your responsibility to bring the glory and dominion of God to that place. This means not backing down, not being a coward, not trying to coexist, not trying to say, "Well, can we all get along?" No, that was for Rodney King. We are for King Jesus, who said:

> *Do not think that I came to bring peace on the earth; I did not come to bring peace, but a sword.*
>
> Matthew 10:34

Jesus was saying: "I am bringing a takeover spirit into my church, and my sons and my daughters are coming in, and they are establishing the kingdom and bringing the glory of my father."

THE MELCHIZEDEK ORDER

What does that mean to be of the Melchizedek order? It means we reign on earth through intercession and decrees through the power of an endless life. From this position, we need not be discouraged. Scripture tells us to pray always and not lose heart.

Let us not lose heart in doing good, for in due time we will reap if we do not grow weary.

Galatians 6:9

Now he was telling them a parable to show that at all times they ought to pray and not lose heart.

Luke 18:1

We will reap...if we do not lose heart.

We are not empowered by temporal constrictions as the Levitical priests were. We are operating in the Spirit of Jesus Christ.

But if the Spirit of Him who raised Jesus from the dead dwells in you, He who raised Christ Jesus from the dead will also give life to your mortal bodies through His Spirit who dwells in you.

Romans 8:11

Notice what this passage tells us. Into what body is God giving life? Our glorified body? The one we get after we leave the earth? No, our mortal body, through Holy Spirit who dwells in us now.

We accomplish things in this life, both in the spirit realm and in the natural realm. What happens in heaven can happen on earth. What is illegal in heaven should be illegal on the earth.

I will give you the keys of the kingdom of heaven; and whatever you bind on earth shall have been bound in heaven, and whatever you loose on earth shall have been loosed in heaven.

Matthew 16:19

This is more than a promise. It is a legal contract. When we function from the Melchizedek priesthood, we grant God legal rights, one of which is to be merciful.

There is a difference, however, between legal and legalistic. Legal is a term used in government. Our Father has a government; it is a kingdom. Under the Levitical priesthood, it was legalistic; it had to be. It was all the people could handle at the time. However, we are no longer in that time.

> But in those sacrifices there is a reminder of sins year by year. For it is impossible for the blood of bulls and goats to take away sins.

Hebrews 10:3-4

Our priesthood starts where the Levitical priesthood left off. It could go no further. Our job as priests is to prepare the world for God's mercy.

One of the reasons we are not seeing the mercy of God throughout the nations of the world is because we are trying to obtain it through a Levitical vein when it was not flowing through that vein. Mercy only flows through a Melchizedek order—a kingdom priesthood order in which Jesus re-established us through his death, burial, resurrection and ascension.

The Father's heart is merciful. He wants to express his heart on the earth but he cannot do so without the priestly anointing on the earth bringing things back into legal order spiritually.

In Genesis 18:17-33, we read of Sodom and Gomorrah. Abraham bargained with God to be merciful to Sodom and Gomorrah, but God could not be merciful because ten righteous people could not be found.

Yet God's heart is merciful. His deepest desire is to show mercy. He only shows judgment as a last resort, and even then, he is yearning to show mercy.

> For we will surely die and are like water spilled on the ground which cannot be gathered up again. Yet God

64

does not take away life, but plans ways so that the banished one will not be cast out from him.

II Samuel 14:14

So, God devises the means for people to receive mercy. How does he do this? Through our intercession.

"I searched for a man among them who would build up the wall and stand in the gap before Me for the land, so that I would not destroy it; but I found no one. Thus I have poured out My indignation on them; I have consumed them with the fire of My wrath; their way I have brought upon their heads," declares the Lord God.

Ezekiel 22:30-31

In this passage, God was looking for someone to build a wall and stand in the gap, but he could not find anybody. Because he could not find anyone, he had to pour out his wrath.

God is looking for one as his intercessor to give him legal right to be merciful. Praise God, someone has been found for us. His name is Jesus, the Christ, the son of the living God.

But if you had known what this means, 'I desire compassion, and not a sacrifice,' you would not have condemned the innocent.

Matthew 12:7

Religion does not want mercy. It cannot convey mercy. Religious people are condemning, judgmental and unforgiving. Everything they say they are, they are not.

God is looking for people who will boldly carry a priestly anointing with intercession so mercy can be brought into the earth. Of course, mercy alone cannot build the kingdom. There is still sin to deal with—not just the act, but the nature. That is where salvation comes in. The ravages of our world: aberrant sexual lifestyles, ruthless oppress, depression, drunkenness and so on will be eradicated, but not through condemnation. You can't convict the sin out of somebody's life. Rejection does not bring people to the altar.

Mercy draws people. Salvation cleanses people. Baptism engrafts people. Grace empowers people. Sonship enlists people.

The Ekklesia is to flow in our priestly anointing to bring things legally in order so God's mercy can come. Our job as a priest to get things legally in place so that we as kings can decree God's will into the nations.

We see this function in this passage of Jesus raising Lazarus from the dead.

> *So they removed the stone. Then Jesus raised His eyes, and said, "Father, I thank You that You have heard Me. I knew that You always hear Me; but because of the people standing around I said it, so that they may believe that You sent Me."*
> *When He had said these things, He cried out with a loud voice, "Lazarus, come forth."*
> *The man who had died came forth, bound hand and foot with wrappings, and his face was wrapped around with a cloth.*
> *Jesus said to them, "Unbind him, and let him go."*

John 11:41-44

Isn't it interesting that the Son of God, who could raise a man from the dead, required that others first roll away the stone, blocking the man's entrance into life? Couldn't Jesus have included the removal of the stone in the miracle? Sure, he could have, but that's not how he works. His power is there; it's available to us. But our job, as kings and priests, is to remove the barrier between the dead and the living—our life-giving, merciful God. That is intercession; that is why we intercede.

1 Peter 2:5

Recall Paul's words to the government officials preparing to torture him, unaware of his citizenship status?

> *The commander ordered [Paul] to be brought into the barracks...[to] be examined by scourging so that he*

might find out the reason why [the Jews] were shouting against him that way. But when they stretched him out with thongs, Paul said to the centurion who was standing by, "Is it lawful for you to scourge a man who is a Roman and uncondemned?"

Acts 22:24-25

Paul knew that legal standing determined what could and could not be done to him, and his challenge stopped them in their tracks.

So, it is with the legal standing in the Spirit. Again:

I will give you the keys of the kingdom of heaven; and whatever you bind on earth shall have been bound in heaven, and whatever you loose on earth shall have been loosed in heaven.

Matthew 16:19

SPIRITUAL SACRIFICES

Our job in this Melchizedek role, this new order of the priesthood, is to offer spiritual sacrifices that we can get things legally in place.

"You also, as living stones, are being built up as a spiritual house for a holy priesthood, to offer up spiritual sacrifices acceptable to God through Jesus Christ."

What are some of the spiritual sacrifices that we need to offer?

Prayer is a spiritual sacrifice.

Return, O Israel, to the Lord your God,
For you have stumbled because of your iniquity.
Take words with you and return to the Lord.
Say to Him, "Take away all iniquity
And receive us graciously,
That we may present the fruit of our lips.

Hosea 14:1-2

Holy Spirit leads us in what to say. Proper words grant God the legal right to be merciful.

> *And when you are praying, do not use meaningless repetition as the Gentiles do, for they suppose that they will be heard for their many words. 8 So do not be like them; for your Father knows what you need before you ask Him.*
>
> Matthew 6:7-8

> *In the same way the Spirit also helps our weaknesses; for we do not know how to pray as we should, but the Spirit Himself intercedes for us with groaning too deep for words.*
>
> Romans 8:26

Prayer is not informing or persuading God. Prayer is working with God to establish God's will on the earth.

Repentance is a spiritual sacrifice. Now, understand that the word *repent* and the word *confess* are different. *Confess* is "to acknowledge." *Repent* is "to change." Confession just says "Yeah, I did it." True repentance says "I'm done doing that."

> *With gentleness correcting those who are in opposition, if perhaps God may grant them repentance leading to the knowledge of the truth, and they may come to their senses and escape from the snare of the devil, having been held captive by him to do his will.*
>
> 2 Timothy 2:25-26

> *Our soul has escaped as a bird*
> *Out of the snare of the trapper*
> *The snare is broken and we have escaped.*
>
> Psalm 124:7

Praise and worship is a spiritual sacrifice. Religion has a song service. Kingdom has a worship service. Religion sings about the King of Kings. Kingdom sings to Him.

> *Through Him then, let us continually offer up a sacrifice of praise to God, that is, the fruit of lips that give thanks to His name.*
>
> Hebrews 13:16

Giving is a spiritual sacrifice. Cornelius was a Roman centurion whose giving and prayers created a memorial.

> *And fixing his [Cornelius'] gaze on [the angel] and being much alarmed, he said, "What is it, Lord?" And [the angel] said to him, "Your prayers and alms have ascended as a memorial before God.*
>
> Acts 10:4

Religion says: "Don't give. They're just after your money." Kingdom says: "Giving establishes a memorial for you, a place of remembrance that brings about the mercy, grace, provision and glory of God."

> *And the priest shall take a handful of the grain offering as its memorial offering and offer it up in smoke on the altar...*
>
> Numbers 5:26

This was a memorial portion that created a voice in heaven that caused God to remember.

CONCLUSION

We, from the Melchizedek priesthood anointing, offer sacrifices that legally grant God the right to be merciful. We grant him the legal right as Judge to fulfill his fatherly passion on the earth.

When we get the Levi stone in place, we are actually putting Melchizedek's stone in that place bearing Levi's name. We are priests through the covenant of Jesus Christ, not through our own doing. We are priests through an endless life.

God is bringing things in order. He brought us into this priesthood to operate not only as priests but also kings. We are to set things legally in order to decree God's will into the realm in which he called us to live and govern.

THE STONE OF JUDAH

Stone-Thrower

HAVE YOU EVER WONDERED WHAT TRIBE YOU ARE FROM? Tribe—as in the 12 tribes of Israel. Just as Jacob had 12 biological sons, and each son formed a tribe with a unique calling, characteristic and purpose, believers today also fall into certain tribes, though they may not be aware of it.

Tribes are important to God. We see in scripture, especially throughout the Old Testament, that God did things through tribes. 1 Kings Chapter 17, 1 Samuel 17 and 1 Kings 18 will show us just that.

This is why, in 1 Kings 18, Elijah rebuilt the altar with 12 stones before the fire of God fell on his sacrifice. As we have discussed, each stone represented a tribe, and from the tribe came a unique contribution to the altar upon which the fire of God fell. It is that altar that we must rebuild today if we are going to see the power of God fall as he has promised.

JUDAH

A derivative meaning of the name *Judah* is often related to *praise*, but it does not mean to *give* praise. It means to *receive* praise. Judah means "to be praised, to give thanks for."

What does it mean to be praised? Well, it does not mean to worship. It means that God looks at your maturity and says: "Good Job! No matter what you are experiencing in warfare around you, I believe in you. I know everything that you have been through. I see the blood on your hands. I see the sweat on your brow. I see the scars in your life, but I believe in you."

A religious spirit cannot handle that concept. "Oh no, no, no. Praise belongs to God."

Well, yes it does, but he can return it wherever he desires. Father will speak into your life and he will identify things that you are doing well in the course of your assignment, just as he will identify things that need corrected. It goes both ways, and it feels great when he says "Well done!"

God is thankful for us. He does nothing in the earth without us. We can do nothing in the earth without him. That is how he set it up. That's why our assignments matter. To each of us: our calling matters, our purpose matters, and whatever area of life that we are working in and functioning in what God's called you to...that also matters.

Judah means "to be thankful for, to make a confession, to be praised, to give thanks for, to make confessions, to be placed in certainty." Often when we think about confession, we apply it only to sin, but this is a confession of joy!

Here is the good news. The fight is fixed! We have been placed in certain victory. See, religion tells us that everything is going to be alright when we get to heaven. In the *sweet by and by*, everything is going to be fine. Let me tell you, everything can be fine right here. And if it's not, something's amiss. Amen!

STONE-THROWERS

Most people know King David and his stories, including his epic fight with Goliath. What is less well-known is that David was of the tribe of Judah. As such, he possesses the qualities of that tribe. Therefore, we can learn much about the characteristics of Judah and the reason Elijah placed the Judah stone as he rebuilt the altar, from David's life.

The principle quality of David is courage.

Then it happened when the Philistine rose and came and drew near to meet David, that David ran quickly toward the battle line to meet the Philistine.

1 Samuel 17:48

Some folks are cowards, just like David's brothers. They praise God when their armor is shiny and there is no fighting going on. They look like fierce warriors, but when the giant starts cursing their God in the valley, they hide behind the rocks.

David didn't hide. He ran towards the battle line. This typifies the characteristics of the tribe of Judah. When Judah is in the right place, they are not afraid of battle. They know that the giant has no authority to defeat them. If you will run to the fight, God will use you at the battle line.

Notice in this passage that David never called the enemy by his name, *Goliath*. Instead, he identified him by his death sentence. David called him an *Uncircumcised Philistine*. David was basically telling him: "You are not a Jew. You don't belong to this tribe. You are not in covenant with God. You are about to have a bad day."

Here's my definition of a bad day:

And David put his hand into his bag and took from it a stone and slung it, and struck the Philistine on his forehead. And the stone sank into his forehead so that he fell on his face to the ground.

1 Samuel 17:49-50

The name *Judah* in Hebrew means "to throw or to cast stones, to stretch forth the hand as one who would throw, to take the sling and throw the stone."

Growing up in the backside of the desert, David had to make a choice: "What am I going to become proficient in? I am here to protect these sheep from things that might eat them or eat me. So, I have to become proficient in something that is going to be used by God in my life to protect me."

I can imagine this truth suddenly dawning on him.

"Whoa! I'm from Judah, the tribe of the stone-throwers. I should get proficient at throwing stones."

Out in the desert alone with just God and the sheep, God was developing him.

His brothers, also of the tribe of Judah, eventually found themselves at war with the Philistines, fighting with spears and shields. They were trying to win battles outside of their identity. That didn't work out so well.

The lesson here is you have to know what tribe you are from, what God's called you to do, and where God has strategically placed you to win battles.

People naturally gravitate to comfort, even in their spiritual lives. Their pursuit of God comes from a place of seeking to make life easier. Yet God has not called us to easy; he has called us to victory after victory as we live in him and for him. We will find our true comfort on the other side of the battle.

David was from the tribe of stone-throwers, but unlike his brothers, he embraced his identity. That is why, when he walked down that mountainside, he had his bag, his sling and a staff in his hand. That staff was a very important piece of David's life. See, when a young boy became a man in that culture, he was not given a car or a deed to property. He was given a staff, and that staff was like a diary. It had things carved in it that belonged to the generations before him. It was a piece of history. Walking down the valley to meet Goliath, David carried his history with God. Hallelujah!

Likewise, when we are facing the hardest times in our lives, we need to have our staffs in hand to feel our history with God because this is where our faith in God is built. And it is God who is going to bring us through the fight.

I am certain David's staff had a bear and a lion carved in it, and it was fixin' to have a very surprised uncircumcised Philistine carved in it as well. *"Is there not a cause?"* David was clearly aggravated with his brothers. In essence, he was saying: "Why are you here hiding behind rocks when you should be out there throwing them?"

David's brothers were hiding behind their purpose. David was calling them to come out from behind the rocks and stop being cowards.

Church people are good at hiding behind our purposes when it should be in front of us, in our hands as instruments of battle. That is when your purpose becomes a tool, not an identity. See, being called to a purpose and acting in that purpose are two different things. Shiny armor looks great...until it's used in battle.

Whenever Judah is in operation, there is a blessing. But whenever we are not handling our purpose correctly, when we are hiding behind the stone instead of wielding it as a weapon, things are out of place. When Judah is out of place in our lives and in the Body of Christ, it means we are missing the target. Instead of weaponizing stones, we get stones thrown at us. We become accustomed to losing battles and hiding like cowards.

When Judah is out of place, we have shame in the place of praise. There is no mercy in other people's judgment, only the fear of giants. As a result, we follow the crowd and hide from the fight.

When Samuel came to Jesse's house to anoint the future king, he saw young men looking very kingly. Unfortunately, they lacked the intestinal fortitude to be king. They didn't have the guts for it; they only looked the part.

Modern Christianity is resplendent in appearances. Yet God is looking for sons and daughters to break the curse of superficiality off the church and rise up to declare they are not afraid of the giants.

In America, we are at a turning point. We are in the worst of times, yet we are in the best of times. We are on the threshold of revival. We will see more people born again, coming out of the darkness and the bondages of their lives, than ever before. Yet there is an uncircumcised giant screaming at America, telling us we are defeated and enslaved as it tries to destroy our history and culture and wipe us off the map.

To hell with that! Judah is rising. God is raising a people in spite of the voices of the giant, the uncircumcised spawn of the devil shouting curses on us.

God is looking for people who will be intentionally prophetic. Yes, we see the evil in front of us, but what is in front of us is not the outcome. We are a strategic piece of the redemption of this nation. We cannot afford to look inwardly, stuck in our own church and ministry and focused solely on our own lives and well-being.

God is shifting the church and the nation. Like David, we are heading into the valley intent on victory, not defeat. You see, the Philistines made a fatal mistake the day they challenged Israel. They took the battle to the land of Judah, the land of the stone-throwers.

They expected an easy fight. They were wrong. I can almost hear them saying "Our modern-day weapons against the measly rock throwers. Hah! We got this!"

America's naysayers are also wrong. God is not done with America. This nation has a destiny and a purpose, and that purpose has not changed. God is raising America up to be a voice of the kingdom to the nations, and he is looking for the Judah in us to stand and declare: "The devil is on my land. We got this. He put his foot in my city. We got this. He said he's going to take over our Statehouse. We got this. He's declared he will have the White House, the Supreme Court. We got this! We are not going to coexist with the devil. We are not going to coexist with Goliath. We are going put a stone right between his damned eyes, take his sword and cut his damned head off while the armies of the Lord flood the battlefield and rout our enemies. The Judah in us will stir the Judah in the Ekklesia." Hallelujah!

When God shifts us, everything changes. We start dreaming differently, hearing differently, prophesying differently. We start seeing things in the spirit as never before. It is normal to wonder what normal is anymore. We are leaving the pasture and entering the battlefield, fighting the good fight not as simple warriors but as kings. We fight as kings! The stakes couldn't be higher. It's not a few sheep anymore; it's the destiny of a nation.

Whenever Judah is in its rightful place, it literally means "proficiency in your gift." When you decide to be a Judah, you will be proficient in your gift. See, David did not carry Saul's armor, even though they tried to dress him up like one of them. He was not like Saul, a Benjamite (we will get to them later). He was a stone-thrower. He was Judah!

When we stand up to battle, we are no longer one of the many hiding behind their purposes rather than advancing them. Remember: we are not trying to get people to heaven; we are trying to get heaven to people.

> *Your kingdom come,*
> *Your will be done*
> *On earth as it is in heaven*

> Matthew 6:10

Change is never easy. As we become proficient in our gifts, our brothers and sisters still hiding behind their gifts may despise us.

Let us stand firm. We are kingdom people. Our prayer is not: *Lord get me out of here. Everything is broken and going to hell.*

That is not who we are. We are of the Father in heaven. Show us the battle line and we will run to it. Public opinion is often the first battleground.

Most people who speak badly about others just want other people's problems to be worse so they can feel better about their own troubles. Don't listen to what the enemy is saying through people. Instead, find your tribe. Find your identity. Find your purpose and you will begin to see proficiency in your gift. You will hit the target. Accusations would not stick to you. There will be mercy over you instead of judgment. Bravery will rise up in you through Holy Spirit like you have never seen before.

We need to be brave because the things we are facing are bigger than ourselves. Remember what God told Joshua when he took command after the death of Moses:

> *Moses My servant is dead; now therefore arise, cross this Jordan, you and all this people, to the land which I am giving to them, to the sons of Israel. Every place on which the sole of your foot treads, I have given it to you, just as I spoke to Moses.*
>
> *Have I not commanded you? Be strong and courageous! Do not tremble or be dismayed, for the Lord your God is with you wherever you go.*
>
> Joshua 1:2-3, 9

God is bringing us to the battle line not for defeat but for victory. It has already been determined. Bravery is replacing shame with praise, with having no fear of giants, with never running from a fight but choosing battles that align with our purpose. We are not to live our lives from the place of struggle and defeat but from the place of the victory of our risen Christ.

> *Greater is He who lives in you the he who is in the world.*
>
> 1 John 4:4

This is key. We do not fight every battle. We fight strategically according to our purpose. There will always be battles, and the enemy wants to distract us with fighting for fighting's sake, but when we fight for things according to our purpose, then we take ground for which God has called us.

David said "There is a cause today. A giant is on my land. Brothers, if you are not going with me, I am going down into the valley alone, yet I am not alone. I have a history with God. I am going to pick five smooth stones and aim for the giant's forehead."

David was a stone-thrower. He was proficient in his gift and he knew exactly which stones to pick to hit a giant. So David reached his hand into his tribe's land, his inheritance, the stream, and he chose. He knew the shape, the weight, the feel of the stones as he picked five, put them in his bag and ran towards the battle line.

Goliath's reaction was curious:

> *Am I a dog, that you come to me with sticks?*

1 Samuel 17:43

Hearing Goliath mocking him, David was possibly thinking to himself: "Yea, you just keep thinking this is a stick. This is my history with God."

David then reached in his bag, took a stone and unleashed his inheritance. As he was spinning his sling, aiming at this ugly giant who is mocking his God, I can hear him screaming in his spirit: "I am of Judah, the tribe of stone-throwers. You are going down!"

After the fall of Goliath, David still had four stones left. Coincidentally, Goliath had four brothers. We can assume David went after them as well. After all, David did not pick up four extra stones for added ballast.

THE LION OF JUDAH

The second notable member of the tribe of Judah—the stone-throwers—is found in John 8:1-11.

> *But Jesus went to the Mount of Olives. Early in the morning He came again into the temple, and all the people were coming to Him; and He sat down and began to teach them. The scribes and the Pharisees brought a woman caught in adultery, and having set her in the center of the court...*

The religious people of that day caught a woman in adultery. Of course, no mention is made of the man who likely instigated the encounter, but that's for another book...perhaps the Book of Life.

Scripture continues in verse 4-7:

> *They said to him, "Teacher, this woman has been caught in the act of adultery in the very act. Now the law of Moses commands us to stone such woman, what then do you say?*

79

*They were saying this, testing Him, so that they might
have grounds for accusing Him. But Jesus stooped down
and with His finger wrote on the ground. But when they
persisted in asking Him, He straightened up, and said to
them, "He who is without sin among you, let him be the
first to throw a stone at her."*

Jesus' actions said it all. He stooped down and wrote something
on the ground. When the accusers persisted, intent on trapping him
with something to accuse him of, he stood up straight and declared:
"He who is without sin cast the first stone." Notice he didn't say *sins*,
as in plural, but *sin*, singular. That is very important to understand.
He was not just saying: "Those of you who have never committed
adultery, throw the first stone." He was also saying: "You who have
never stolen from God because you did not tithe, or who have never
lusted, lied, schemed or compromised, you throw the first stone."

Literally, Jesus was saying: "Those of you whose covenant
relationship with the Father is perfect, feel free to throw stones."

And this, from the Lion of Judah, of the tribe of stone-throwers!

*Again He stooped down and wrote on the ground.
When they heard it, they began to go out one by one,
beginning with the older ones...*

Obviously, not one of the accusers passed the test. They had
enough sense to know the state of their relationship with God.

*...and he was left alone with the woman, where she was
in the center of the court.*

Notice that she was still standing in the middle of the court
waiting to be judged, in a place that she could be accused and
stoned.

In verses 10-11,

*Jesus said to her, "Woman, where are they? Did no one
condemn you?" She said, "No one, Lord." And Jesus
said, "I do not condemn you, either. Go. From now on
sin no more."*

In other words: *Have no separation from God any longer.*

Jesus was from the tribe of Judah, the son of David, of the tribe of stone-throwers. Each tribe had certain responsibilities to carry out in the nation of Israel. One of Judah's responsibilities as the tribe that threw stones was to be the ones who stoned condemned people. It was not legal for just anybody to stone. It was Judah's responsibility to carry out punishment.

The religious leaders knew Jesus was of the tribe Judah and so, they brought this case worthy of stoning to him to trap him.

The scribes and Pharisees were saying: "Hey Jesus, you need to live out who you are supposed to be. This woman is caught in adultery, in the very act! And we put her here in the center of the court and Moses' law says we have to stone her. What say ye, *stone thrower*?"

In response to their prodding, Jesus stooped down and wrote in the dirt. I do not know what he wrote. He could have spelled *Judah*. Maybe he underlined it, drew an asterisk, an arrow or wrote #no1stoned2day.

I don't know, but Jesus' message essentially told them: "You are not from Judah. I am from Judah. You do not get to decide when stones are thrown. I decide that. That is my identity and my purpose. Drop your stones or I'll pick up mine. We are not throwing stones today. We are releasing mercy."

See, when you know who you are, you are secure in your identity and purpose in the Father. You have the ability to execute judgment when you need to and release mercy when you need to.

This poor woman was guilty under the law, but Jesus said to her accusers: "Let's look at *your* lives. Why are you trying to illegally be something you're not? Why are you trying to hijack my tribe, step into my responsibility?"

Religion tries to dictate how you are supposed to live out your identity and purpose, how to live your tribe when they are from another tribe. Religion wants to tell you how you do your job.

You're supposed to be angry. You are supposed to be mad. You are supposed to judge the world right now.

You're supposed to be mad at all those rioters, at Black Lives Matter protestors and All Lives Matter protestors, at white men (if you are black), at black men (if you are white), at males (if you are female), at females (if you are males), at the establishment (if you are poor), or the poor (if you are established).

Jesus' redemptive message is still true today: We are not here to throw stones but instead to release mercy in place of judgment. We have a redemptive purpose within us. Hallelujah!

In wrath remember mercy.

Habakkuk 3:2

The world wants you to engage in its rhetoric and embrace its religious and political agendas. It wants to pull you out of your identity. Our job is not to throw stones at one another but to bring healing and deliverance and release mercy instead of judgment.

Blessed are the merciful, for they shall receive mercy.

Matthew 5:7

Mature sons and daughters know when to cast stones and when to gather stones together. In Jesus' name!

Jesus knew he was anointed but he also knew he had authority. That's why the religious leaders hated him. Religion doesn't care if you are anointed; go ahead and shout a little and preach a little. But when you step into authority, you shift the kingdoms of this world to become the kingdoms of our God. That's when it gets real.

CONCLUSION

We are in a decade of the roar of the Lion of the tribe of Judah, a time when his mature sons and daughters, his Ekklesia, are going to roar louder than ever before over America and the nations of the world.

We are going to see darkness exposed. The upheaval in our country is not because the enemy is strong; it is because he is scared; he is exposed. The light has come to expose the darkness. Darkness is getting weaker and it's playing its last card. Not its best card, but its last card.

It is time that you and I, as the Ekklesia of God, the legislative arm of heaven, stand up to the enemy and declare: "This is the law of the land; this belongs to the Kingdom of God; this is how it is going to go and we pull you down in Jesus name. Oh...and if you don't act right, we know how to throw stones...accurately...forcefully.

> *They overcame him by the blood of the lamb and the word of their testimony; they did not love their lives so much as to shrink from death.*
>
> *Therefore rejoice, you heavens and you who dwell in them! But woe to the earth and the sea, because the devil has gone down to you. He is filled with fury, because he knows that his time is short.*
>
> Revelation 12:11-12

THE STONE OF DAN

Judgement

ELIJAH'S PURPOSE IN REBUILDING THE ALTAR WAS NOT FOR HIM; it was to turn Israel's heart back to God. Everything he did was for the people of Israel. He knew what God could do. That's why he challenged the demonic prophets. This is why he mocked them when Baal didn't answer. That's why he asked God to send fire. He was confident that everything that he had done was according to the word of the Lord.

Today, we face similar contests. We are challenging the false prophets who are openly or secretly in league with evil. We have stepped across the threshold for an awakening. God is giving us keys—kingdom principles to restore the altar so his fire can fall. Supernatural acts will convince the people that God is the Lord and that they must turn their hearts to him. Nations are turning to the Lord and seeing the power of God in many different ways.

A critical piece in the rebuilding of the altar is the stone of Dan, representing the tribe of Dan. Dan was a governing tribe. They governed as judges. One of the most famous judges of the tribe of Dan was Samson, although he had his struggles (as did the rest of the tribe).

Fundamentally, *Dan's* name means "to judge, judgment or he who judges, to govern." The prime root of this word means "to rule by implication, to strive as at law."

Notice that it doesn't mean "to strive to work hard," but rather "to strive as at the law." The context is: "I'm using the law to build

85

my case so I can have judgment on my behalf." Another way to put it is: "to contend, to execute judgment, to minister judgment or to plead the cause."

We know from John 16 that our helper is Holy Spirit. The Greek word for *helper* is *paraclete*, as in "one who is called along my side to plead my cause." It is a legal term applicable to the judicial system of heaven. Restoring the stone of Dan to its place in the altar restores the judicial system of heaven to bring about righteous judgments for God on the earth.

TRIBE OF DAN

The tribe of Dan was the last to receive their inheritance among all the tribes of Israel. Aside from being judges, they provided substantial military support for the Kingdom of Israel and were considered experts at war. They were also a seafaring people engaged in travel and commerce.

Now, in the list of the tribes from the Book of Revelation, Dan is not mentioned with the other tribes, but that is for another study. For this book, we are focused on the judicial aspects of the tribe of Dan.

Jacob, in his prophetic blessing over the tribe of Dan, represents it under the notion of a serpent in a path.

> *Dan shall be a serpent in the way,*
> *A horned snake in the path,*
> *That bites the horse's heels,*
> *So that his rider falls backward.*

> Genesis 49:17

So, they're pictured as a snake in the middle of a road that bites at the heel of a horse, making the horse rare up and tossing the rider. Not the kind of people you'd want to mess with.

When Moses blessed the 12 tribes of Israel, he said of Dan:

> *Dan is a lion's whelp,*
> *That leaps forth from Bashan.*

> Deuteronomy 33:22

86

That might not sound like a compliment, but the word *bashan* means "fruitfulness." So, this was saying that Dan was going to leap from a place of fruitfulness. Further, the Jewish interpreters observed that Bashan was a place frequented by lions who would go into all the land looking for their prey. By this statement, then, Moses was pointing out the strength and prowess of this tribe as they extended their territories through a predatory lifestyle. And indeed, they did

We don't know much more about the tribe of Dan, but we see in the Book of Judges that the tribe was often up to no good. For starters, they did not secure the original portion of land that was allotted to them. Instead, Dan migrated North.

> *The territory of the sons of Dan proceeded beyond them; for the sons of Dan went up and fought with Leshem and captured it. Then they struck it with the edge of the sword and possessed it and settled in it; and they called Leshem Dan after the name of Dan their father.*
>
> Joshua 19:47

It appears from this scripture that the portion originally assigned to Dan was insufficient in their eyes. In God's eyes, their land was sufficient, but Dan was not satisfied. Instead, they went to war against Leshem and took that land, adding to their territory.

This is very important as we begin to discover and understand why this stone is out of place.

> *Then the Amorites forced the sons of Dan into the hill country, for they did not allow them to come down to the valley.*
>
> Judges 1:34

> *In those days there was no king of Israel; and in those days the tribe of the Danites was seeking an inheritance for themselves to live in, for until that day an*

inheritance had not been allotted to them as a possession among the tribes of Israel.

Judges 18:1

As the last tribe to get land, they were dissatisfied with what was given to them and did not properly settle the land that God gave them. Instead, they begin to look northward for other lands that seemed more fitting in their own eyes. People in general did things that were right in their own eyes in those days. In essence, they were their own judges.

Dan worshipped other gods, built temples to them and tried to establish another priesthood, which was illegal, of course. Considering this was the tribe who was supposed to be judges, it's evident that they were doing much harm. Corruption in a judicial system brings all kinds of evil and unrighteousness into the land.

The sons of Dan set up for themselves the graven image; and Jonathan, the son of Gershom, the son of Manasseh, he and his sons were priests to the tribe of the Danites until the day of the captivity of the land. So they set up for themselves Micah's graven image which he had made, all the time that the house of God was at Shiloh.

Judges 18:30-31

So the king consulted, and made two golden calves, and he said to them, "It is too much for you to go up to Jerusalem; behold your gods, O Israel, that brought you up from the land of Egypt." He set one in Bethel, and the other he put in Dan.

1 Kings 12:28-29

The tribe later joined Jeroboam in idolatry when the Kingdom of Israel was divided. Apparently, the stone of Dan was out long before Elijah restored it.

The prime root of *Dan* is: "to rule by implication, to judge, to strive as at the law." It means "to contend." This is important. The Bible tells us we need to contend for the faith.

CONTEND

Contend is a very powerful word. Studies into the derivations of this word reveal a picture of a boxer fighting in the ring.

> *Fight the good fight of faith; take hold of the eternal life to which you were called, and you made the good confession in the presence of many witnesses.*

> 1 Timothy 6:12

Today, we need to contend for our nation, for the vision and the purpose that God has for us. We need to be people who say, "No, we won't give up. We're going to stand and contend. We're going to take what Dan threw away and we're going to redeem it." We need to contend, and we need to win.

> *But in all these things we overwhelmingly conquer through Him who loved us.*

> Romans 8:37

Jesus died; we died with him. He rose; we rose with him. He sat at the right hand of the Father; we are seated in heavenly places with Christ Jesus right now, ruling and reigning.

> *[God] raised us up with Him, and seated us with Him in the heavenly places in Christ Jesus*

> Ephesians 2:6

This makes us more than conquerors. When the enemy comes against us, we're not weak. We're not idle in the ring. We are contenders for the fight. We are contenders for the ground that God's given us and that we have taken for God in the expansion of his kingdom.

JUDGES

Recall that Dan's name means "to judge." Further derivations include: "to govern, strive, act as judge." As Isaiah wrote:

For the Lord is our judge,
The Lord is our lawgiver,
The Lord is our king;
He will save us.

Isaiah 33:22

This passage of the scripture was a major influence that the founders of America used to establish this nation with our three parts of government.

- *The Lord is our judge*—our Judicial System.
- *The Lord is our lawgiver*—our Congress.
- *The Lord is our King*—our executive branch.

So, why does God want judges? Doesn't Jesus say in Matthew 7:1, *"Do not judge so that you will not be judged."* Then why is God referred to as a judge?

The word *judge* in this scripture is the same word as *Dan* in the Hebrew. It refers to righteous judgments, the ability (and right) to approach the throne of God to receive judgments on our behalf.

Has God called us to judge? Yes, he has. Holy Spirit came to establish us in the fact that the prince of this world has been judged.

And concerning judgment, because the ruler of this world has been judged.

John 16:11

Judgment is a huge part of the Kingdom of God. When Dan's stone is out of place, we get wrong judgments or we are forced to surrender the judgments given to us by God to the enemy. Thus, we have no victory in our lives. The enemy is out to spoil those righteous judgments and keep us from walking them out in our lives.

THE JUDICIAL SYSTEM

Judgement is vital to spiritual warfare, and yet this has been taught incorrectly in most churches. Ironically, the church has prided itself in its execution of spiritual warfare. We have books, conferences, songs, even dances focused on warfare. The only thing we don't have is...victory. Spiritual warfare can stir the prophetic but it produces little else. Why?

The issue is that we have not discerned where our battles really lie and how God intended for us to fight that good fight of faith. Consider this passage from the book of Daniel:

> *I kept looking*
> *Until thrones were set up,*
> *And the Ancient of Days took His seat;*
> *His vesture was like white snow*
> *And the hair of His head like pure wool.*
> *His throne was ablaze with flames,*
> *Its wheels were a burning fire.*
> *A river of fire was flowing*
> *And coming out from before Him;*
> *Thousands upon thousands were attending Him,*
> *And myriads upon myriads were standing before Him;*
> *The court sat,*
> *And the books were opened.*

Daniel 7:9-10

Notice: *"The court sat."* What court?

A court represents a judicial system, one with judges, judgments, books, precedence from previous judgements. Prayer is also an important part of this. Prayer is an activity that takes place in the judicial system of heaven.

Prayer is not a religious word. Prayer is a judicial word, a legal word. If you've ever been to court, it's possible that you've heard a lawyer say, "We pray the court...." This is a legal term that we find operational in a judicial system. There are also petitions, accusations, arguments, protocol and evidence. Remarkably, this applies to the judicial system of heaven just as it does the judicial system of earth.

Scripture reveals that the place of initial conflict is the judicial system of heaven, not the battlefield of spiritual warfare. This is why the first place of intercession should be through the judicial system.

This is why it is imperative that we get the stone of Dan back in its place. It all starts with judgement.

Most Christians believe that when we pray, we're praying on a battlefield. Consequently, they rush into conflict without securing a verdict from heaven. This leads to chaos, backlash and destruction in their lives from satanic forces.

Before going onto the battlefield, we must establish a legal precedence to be there in the first place. Rushing in and yelling at the devil, making wild decrees and pronouncements do more of stirring up demonic forces than they do dismantling them. This will not lead to victory. Prayer and warfare should not be a shot in the dark. We should be able to pinpoint the things we seek with great accuracy. We are not shooting blindly.

God does everything decently and in order. This is why we must move into the judicial system of heaven first and the battlefield second.

JESUS AND THE JUDICIAL SYSTEM OF HEAVEN

And I saw heaven opened, and behold, a white horse, and He who sat on it is called Faithful and True, and in righteousness He judges and wages war.

Revelation 19:11

This verse presents many things to us. First, there is an open heaven. We have access to the heavens. From the time that Jesus was baptized in the Jordan River, that voice "out of the heavens" has been speaking to us.

And a voice came out of the heavens: "You are My beloved Son, in You I am well-pleased."

Mark 1:11

Again, on the Mount of Transfiguration:

Then a voice came out of the cloud, saying, "This is My Son, My Chosen One; listen to Him!"

Luke 9:35

92

"Out of the cloud" refers to the heavens being opened.

Remarkably, we find no record of the heavens ever being closed. Certainly, there were times in the Old Testament when they were shut up and made of brass. Yet in the New Covenant, after Jesus was spoken over by the Father, heaven was opened and remains so to this day.

> And I saw heaven opened, and behold, a white horse, and He who sat on it is called Faithful and True, and in righteousness He judges and wages war.
>
> Revelation 19:11

Notice the order of actions: *"He judges and wages war."* To make war, a verdict must be rendered concerning a situation. We must learn to make war based only on judgments, decisions and verdicts that are rendered within the judicial system of heaven.

Have you ever had prayers that you knew were the will of God and yet they went unanswered? It means that things are legally out of place. The enemy has something against you in the judicial system of heaven when certain prayers go unanswered.

Jesus, teaching on prayer in Matthew 6 and Luke 11 and 18, never placed prayer on a battlefield. Instead, he spoke of prayer flowing from a relationship with the Father, as a friend approaching a friend.

> In a certain city there was a judge who did not fear God and did not respect man. There was a widow in that city, and she kept coming to him, saying, 'Give me legal protection from my opponent.' For a while he was unwilling; but afterward he said to himself, 'Even though I do not fear God nor respect man, yet because this widow bothers me, I will give her legal protection, otherwise by continually coming she will wear me out.'" And the Lord said, "Hear what the unrighteous judge said; now, will not God bring about justice for His elect who cry to Him day and night, and will He delay long

over them? I tell you that He will bring about justice for them quickly.

Luke 18:1-8

Jesus, in this passage, is teaching us that when we pray, we are entering into a judicial system to get a verdict. Remember, prayer is a legal term, and a judicial system can only render verdicts according to testimony given. That's why it tells us in the Book of Revelation 12:11:

They overcame him because of the blood of the Lamb and because of the word of their testimony.

Now, the word of your testimony is not about how bad you were before salvation. Rather, it comes from your book in heaven. In heaven's judicial system there is a counsel and books. The books represent things that are predestined or dreamed for you by God. We get glimpses into things God has written in our book.

And in Your book were all written
The days that were ordained for me

Psalm 139:16

Our testimony is what God says about us, not what the enemy produced in us. Testimonies such as:

- I am more than a conqueror through him that loved me and gave himself for me.
- I can do all things through Jesus Christ who gives me strength.
- I have the power to trample on the heads of serpents and scorpions and all the power of the enemy.
- Nothing by any means shall harm me.
- Greater is he that is in me than he that is in the world.

We get our verdicts according to our testimony given. We make the case that gives God the legal right to release his father's heart in our lives.

If things are legally out of order, we must step into the office of priest to get things legally in order. Then we can step into the kingly anointing to release the decrees. Those decrees are the verdicts that God gives us according to our testimony and the case that we present. Remember, God only does things on the earth when he can find a person to do it through. We saw in the chapter on the stone of Levi that God was looking for a person to stand in the gap. He needs people of the earth to release decrees in the kingly anointing because he cannot release his father's heart in this judicial system without his position as a righteous judge being satisfied.

We need to get Dan's stone back in place and get the judge back in his seat so righteous decrees can be released as we present our case to God for ourselves, our family, our region and our nation.

HINDRANCES

Three things will hinder the Kingdom of God from coming into the earth through you.

1. Sin

We must move into new realms of holiness and consecration because the enemy can use our sin to resist us. I'm not referring to holiness in the legalistic term with regulations and ritual observances. *Holiness* means "separated unto." We're not separated *from sin*; we're separated *unto God*. When trying to avoid sin, you're going to miss the mark every time. Holiness is being separated unto God, realizing that you are his, he is yours, and that you belong to him. Holiness is not based on what you do; it is based on what he's done. That's why God could say:

> For I am the Lord your God. Consecrate yourselves therefore, and be holy, for I am holy.
>
> Leviticus 11:44

2. Bloodline

We need to cleanse the bloodline. We have to answer the sins of our father so the enemy can't use them to build a case against us. Having our bloodline cleansed by the blood of the lamb is so important.

Be of sober spirit, be on the alert. Your adversary, the devil, prowls around like a roaring lion, seeking someone to devour.

1 Peter 5:8

The devil is opportunistic.

You shall not worship [idols] or serve them; for I, the Lord your God, am a jealous God, visiting the iniquity of the fathers on the children, and on the third and the fourth generations of those who hate Me.

Deuteronomy 5:9

This scripture tells us that sin can visit us back by four generations. This is why we need to ask God what is in our bloodline that needs to be cleansed. We can know some of those things by how our father acted, our grandfather acted, our great grandfather acted. Then learn what needs to be repented of, what needs to be confessed and what needs to be cleansed.

3. Motives

God judges the heart, so our motives are important. Satan can build a case against us based on our motives just as he did against Job based on his motives for serving God.

Then Satan answered the Lord, "Does Job fear God for nothing? Have You not made a hedge about him and his house and all that he has, on every side? You have blessed the work of his hands, and his possessions have increased in the land. But put forth Your hand now and touch all that he has; he will surely curse You to Your face."

Job 1:9-11

Satan had permission to test Job. Yet Job could bring about a righteous answer to prove what Satan had said was wrong.

The motives of our hearts must be pure so that the enemy has no ammunition to bring accusations against us in the judicial system of heaven.

KEYS FOR JUDICIAL VICTORY

Never address the adversary.

Only speak to the judge. Around the throne of God, our adversary has been stripped of his power. We must deal with him legally. We don't go into a courtroom, look at the accuser and say, "You're wrong. You don't know what you're talking about. I bind you up in the name of Jesus. I don't receive what you're saying against me."

You won't win that way. The accuser has no power to acquit you. He has no power to free you. He has no power to release you from the accusations, charges, or complaints that have been brought against you. In fact, he wants those things to stick.

You address the judge. The judge is the one who has the power to free you and give you a righteous judgment.

When you get the verdict against your adversary, he becomes of no consequence regardless of what he says or does. His words carry no more power.

THE VERDICT

Adhere to God's verdicts.

God's verdicts are the words of God, the promises of God, the prophetic words that he has given you over your life.

> *This command I entrust to you, Timothy, my son, in accordance with the prophecies previously made concerning you, that by them you fight the good fight.*
>
> 1 Timothy 1:18

Paul is speaking to Timothy about verdicts from his book. They're God's words, dreams and will for his life.

When the enemy tries to take your righteous verdict, you can hold up the judgment from the court, the word of God, the prophetic word, the promise of God, and you can render the enemy helpless.

<u>Kings decree.</u>

Kings do not intercede. They're not on that side of the bench. They are enthroned. In Daniel 7:9, it says, *"Thrones (plural) were set up, and the Ancient of Days took His seat."* There are more thrones than you could imagine.

As kings, we sit in a place of decreeing as kings. When we get things legally in place as priests through intercession and answering every accusation against us, we can shift anointings and decree as kings the righteous judgment into the earth.

The Bible says in Job 22:28, *"You will also decree a thing, and it will be established for you."*

We present our case to the judge, not the adversary. When the judge renders a verdict for us, because we overcome by the blood of the lamb and the word of our testimony, now that righteous judgment is in our hands. We can step into our kingly anointing and decree things that will be established.

<u>Expect answers quickly</u>.

We can expect answers to come quickly when we move off the battlefield and into the judicial system of heaven. When I did this, answers to prayers I'd been struggling with for years came to me. All of my warring, yelling and petitioning hadn't brought things that I knew God wanted to bring to me from heaven. But when I learned to navigate the judicial system of heaven, things happened quickly. My adversaries were silenced and I was avenged speedily like the woman in Luke 18.

When things are done in order, answers come quickly.

OUT OF PLACE

When Dan's stone is out of place, we get unrighteous judgments, judges and rulings. We have accusations made against us that we cannot answer. Laws are enacted that produce evil. There is no spirit to contend for what the kingdom of heaven is desiring to release into the earth. There is a disconnect from God, our righteous judge.

The enemy develops a stronghold in our nation when there are no righteous judgments. We are unable to get breakthroughs to see things vindicated in a legal matter through the judicial system of heaven. Frustrated, we often wind up taking the law into our own hands and become lawless. Thus, there is a false priesthood enacted in the land when Dan's stone is out of place.

We've seen many unrighteous judgments in our nation. That's why the courts are so important. We need righteous judges in our land. Some judges on the Supreme Court of the United States interpret the law to fit their agenda. They brought about abortion. They legalized murder in the latter years of someone's life by calling it *death by dignity* or *assisted suicide*. They're releasing judgments against people who want to worship God. They target things in our nation that bring about the demise of our nation. It is amazing how five out of nine people can shift the destiny and purpose of a nation by just making decisions and calling them legal when they're actually illegal and certainly ungodly.

We need God to move. We need the stone of Dan back in place. This is not a religious thing. This is a kingdom thing.

God is concerned about our courts. God loves our legal system. He wants righteous men and women on those benches. He created the Ekklesia that brings about the will of God on the earth, releasing righteous judgment and legislation.

CONCLUSION

God has a kingdom, not a religion, and that kingdom government wants to see righteousness released in the nation. This is why it is so important that we see righteous people sitting in these judicial seats in our nations. God is getting us ready to shift those courts. We're in a new era. God is giving the church a window of opportunity to pray in such a way that we see righteous judges on the Supreme Court.

A trusted leader and intercessor, Apostle Ken Malone, had a dream about the Supreme Court in which the Chief Justice said:

"We're being overrun, we need reinforcements."

Ken's answer?

"Damn the torpedoes. We're coming."

We're coming with righteous judgment from heaven. We're coming with the righteousness of God to vindicate what God has in his heart for the nation. As we pray and fast and hear from God, we're going to see Heaven's judicial system shift America's courts! We're going to see a judicial system redeemed in the nations and righteous people in those seats.

We must stop shouting at the Devil. We must comprehend our standing in the judicial system of heaven and speak directly to the righteous judge—our heavenly Father. We're bringing spiritual warfare back in order—the judicial first and then the battlefield.

What happens when Dan's stone gets in place?

The righteous judges take their seats.

The books of heaven are opened up and the righteous judge begins to read from those books the things that he put there that were in his heart.

We begin to leap from Bashan, a place of fruitfulness.

The spirit of the contender rises up in the Ekklesia.

We don't give in and we don't give up and we don't give out. Praise God.

We execute the Lord's judgment according to Psalms 149:7-8.

> *To execute vengeance on the nations*
> *And punishment on the peoples,*
> *To bind their kings with chains*
> *And their nobles with fetters of iron,*
> *To execute on them the judgment written;*
> *This is an honor for all His godly ones.*
> *Praise the Lord!*

THE STONE OF NAPHTALI

Wrestler

So Rachel said, "With mighty wrestlings I have wrestled with my sister, and I have indeed prevailed." And she named him Naphtali.

Genesis 30:8

In Genesis, we read that Rachel was wrestling with her sister. I imagine that she felt like her entire life was a struggle. Recall that she was the second wife to Jacob. He was tricked by her father into first marrying her older sister, Leah, even though he loved Rachel. This setup a powerful dynamic between the three of them that persisted through their lifetimes.

Rachel struggled with Leah over who could have the most children for Jacob and so possess his heart. The competition grew so fierce over the years that both sisters eventually gave Jacob their maids for wives as well. Jacob wound up with four women bearing his children instead of two. You might wonder how that all worked out? (That's for another book.)

Whenever Leah (or her maid) gave birth, she rejoiced because her husband would stay with her. Note her joy after giving birth to Zebulun:

Then Leah said, "God has endowed me with a good gift; now my husband will dwell with me, because I have borne him six sons." So she named him Zebulun.

Genesis 30:20

And so Jacob did stay with her...for a season. Then he went back to his other wives, as was their custom.

This was the dynamic among the family when Rachel's maid gave birth to Naphtali. She felt that she had gotten a victory over her sister, which is why Naphtali's name means "my wrestling, to twine together." Think of the scripture in Ecclesiastes:

And if one can overpower him who is alone, two can resist him. A cord of three strands is not quickly torn apart.

Ecclesiastes 4:12

Further derivations of Naphtali are: "self forward, to show self in the past, to show yourself unsavory to wrestle, to show oneself astute."

The word *astute* means "to be mentally sharp, to be clever." It refers to a thought process that enables us to navigate through sticky situations, opinions and narratives. These are important qualities today when faced with a barrage of information—some of it actually based on current realities—that the narrative-driven media blasts at us 24/7.

The word *astute* also means "shrewdness." It refers to an ability to notice and understand things clearly. We could also call this *discernment*. Not just a spiritual discernment, but a natural ability to discern as well. It is something you and I need to be able to get the stone back in its rightful place in order to see the fire of God fall. When this stone is out of place, there is no discernment, no ability to fight or wrestle, no ability to notice and understand things clearly.

Being astute implies that if there are two narratives coming at you from opposing viewpoints (or agendas), you are able to extract the truth. It is important. When we find truth, we find Jesus. Truth makes us free (John 8:32)!

> *Jesus said to him, "I am the way, and the truth, and the life; no one comes to the Father but through Me.*

Truth is important. It is the key to victory. Not your truth or my truth but the truth of God—the Truth of all truths. It is said that there are two sides to every story, but there are really three. There is my side, your side and then there is the truth. So when we are discerning things, it is not to promote our agendas but to promote the will of God.

In handling truth, we must be ruthless. Anything in our culture that does not line up with the Kingdom of God must be expelled from our lives. In the Kingdom of God, opinions do not matter unless they are aligned with God's truth.

Even in the church among the saints, we are eager, even passionate, to give our opinion. However, as we mature, we grow to the place where we can lay down our own opinions on the altar of truth. The fact is, our opinions are often a product of our culture, and so we tend to filter truth through these biases.

Laying down our opinions is not easy, nor is it comfortable. This is why we must be intentional about it. It can feel disloyal to those who raised us or the environment that fostered us. Yet that was our starting point; it is not our finishing point. We must be willing to know God's truth, Kingdom truth and the truth comes from Jesus. Further, we must be willing to *move* into truth—not our truth; God's truth.

When we are astute, we understand things clearly and with mental sharpness, cleverness and wisdom.

> *Wisdom is the principal thing;*
> *Therefore get wisdom;*
> *Yea, with all thy getting,*
> *Get understanding.*

Proverbs 4:7 ASV

Without truth and understanding in our lives, we are helpless.

To be astute also means "having or showing an ability to accurately assess situations or people and to turn this to one's advantage." As an astute business person, for example, you are able to hear what potential customers are saying about you, your products and your presentation, and this is vital to success.

So, when we get Naphtali's stone back in place, we become astute and successful. We have the ability to notice and understand things clearly with mental sharpness.

When I was a police officer, we often came upon situations for which we had limited information, and most of that information was given by victims from their perspective. We knew that when we arrived on the scene, it could be totally different than what we ever imagined. We had to be ready for that. Skillful policing meant we had to assess the situation correctly.

As believers, we must do the same thing. We must assess situations and people correctly because if we don't, we will move in our own opinions, ideas and culture, and we will miss God. Ironically, because our own ways seem right to us, we will think (erroneously) that God's favor is on our thoughts and actions because they feel natural to us.

Now, God knows we are biased and that we filter everything through experience and culture. That's why Holy Spirit gives us gifts like the word of wisdom or knowledge. This is the beginning of the prophetic, enabling us to see into things and minister to people to bring them into God's will for their lives.

So, to understand what Naphtali really means, we have to understand the culture and the circumstances involved in his naming. Rachel had been wrestling with her sister and felt she had gained an advantage through the boy's birth. Also, Jacob spoke a blessing regarding his son:

> *Naphtali is a doe let loose,*
> *He gives beautiful words.*

Genesis 49:21

A doe is a deer, a female deer, and man can they run! (Especially when I'm hunting them.) They are beautiful when they dance in the field.

Recall that Naphtali's meaning includes: "to wrestle, to twist, to twine a three-fold cord."

Wrestling was a family tradition. Naphtali must have gotten some of that wrestling tendency from his father, Jacob, who was tenacious. He worked 14 years for his two wives. He endured the constant scheming and trickery of his father-in-law, Laban, who changed his wages 10 times over their years together, and he constantly swapped out the good livestock with the poor livestock. And whenever Jacob would get the upper hand, which was frequently because God blessed him, Laban tried another means to rob him. Yet Jacob, through God, always prevailed.

Even though *Jacob's* name means "deceiver, supplanter, and manipulator," he was able to take hold of something and hang on to it until he got what he wanted out of it. He even tricked his older brother, Esau, out of his birthright, something that would haunt him later in life.

THE JOURNEY

After years of struggle with Laban, God told Jacob it was time to move on.

> *I am the God of Bethel, where you anointed a pillar, where you made a vow to Me; now arise, leave this land, and return to the land of your birth.*

Genesis 31:13

And so, Jacob's journey began. The word *Bethel* means "house of God." Jacob's journey to the place of his birth was to get back to his identity, to find out who he was and to erase his past. This would not be an easy journey; there would be many growth opportunities masquerading as challenges.

Scripture says we do not wrestle against flesh and blood, and this was true of Jacob on this journey. On his way to discover his identity, God spoke to him at Bethel. He heard God but had not yet encountered him. And yet, as we shall see, entering the house of God was not enough for Jacob to obtain his identity, destiny or purpose. It was not enough to *qualify* him to step into who God called him to be. And it is not enough for us today.

Of course, some people think that everybody is approved by God because whoever will call on the name of the Lord will be saved (ref. Romans 10:13). Right? Yes, but that doesn't always mean what we want it to mean. The Bible says: *"For many are called, but few are chosen"* (Matthew 22:14). The Bible is telling us that while some choose to mature and grow up, many others want to be babies and get spoon-fed all their lives.

So yes, Jacob was on a journey through Bethel, but there was really no change to him other than increasing his frustration and fear. His father in law, Laban, pursued him and Jacob had to make peace with him (ref. Genesis 31). He also encountered angels (ref. Genesis 32:1). Yet there were bigger things in store for Jacob.

WRESTLING WITH GOD

The house of God is a good place to find God, but finding him there in a corporate experience is not enough to change your name, find your purpose, encounter your destiny and pull fear and religion out of your heart. See, even at this time, Jacob was not sure who his God was going to be or what this God could do. Recall the beginning of Jacob's relationship with God.

> Then Jacob made a vow, saying, "If God will be with me and will keep me on this journey that I take, and will give me food to eat and garments to wear, and I return to my father's house in safety, then the Lord will be my God. This stone, which I have set up as a pillar, will be God's house, and of all that You give me I will surely give a tenth to You."

Genesis 28:20-22

"Then the Lord will be my God." Really? I'm sure God was impressed when Jacob gave him permission to be his God. Little did he know, but Jacob was about to meet God in a big way. As is typical of life-changing encounters with God, it happened when he was alone.

> *Then Jacob was left alone, and a man wrestled with him until daybreak. When he saw that he had not prevailed against him, he touched the socket of his thigh; so the socket of Jacob's thigh was dislocated while he wrestled with him. Then he said, "Let me go, for the dawn is breaking." But he said, "I will not let you go unless you bless me." So he said to him, "What is your name?" And he said, "Jacob." He said, "Your name shall no longer be Jacob, but Israel; for you have striven with God and with men and have prevailed."*
>
> *Then Jacob asked him and said, "Please tell me your name." But he said, "Why is it that you ask my name?" And he blessed him there. So Jacob named the place Peniel, for he said, "I have seen God face-to-face, yet my life has been preserved."*

Genesis 32:24-30

Now, we understand that this word *man* is literally the word *ish*, which means a representation of God—a spirit man. So, a spirit man wrestled with Jacob until daybreak. At the end, God touched the socket of Jacob's thigh and it was dislocated and Jacob was never himself again.

The word *blessed* means many things. For one, it means "that in blessing me, you bless everybody." It also means "to congratulate." Think about the exchange between Jacob and God.

"Congratulate me."

"Wait a minute. Your thigh is out of the socket. You are not who you were. You are losing the fight."

"Yeah, but I am not letting you go until you congratulate me and I get what I came for. You must bless me and bring me into a place to where I am living as who I am supposed to be because I cannot go on like this any longer"

So *congratulate* also involves boasting. Can you imagine wrestling with God and God says, "Look, I have to go. The sun is coming up. I am going to touch you here. You are done."

But you hang on and say, "I am not letting you go until you congratulate me as the winner."

Amazing.

Blessed also means "to persist in blessing." Jacob wanted God to speak over him. *Jacob's* name meant: "supplanter, deceiver, schemer, cunning." So he was saying: "I want my blessing. My grandfather had a blessing. My father had a blessing. I must have a blessing because I am going into the land where my brother lives and he does not like me too well. I am not letting you go until you bless me."

Finally, the word *blessed* also means "to salute."

Wow! It is one thing to congratulate but it is another thing to salute. A salute would bring a sense of seniority. Consider what God did to man in the beginning. He gave us seniority on the earth. He gave us the ability to be kings in the earth. He gave us Kingdom.

God saluted us, saying: "We bless them. They are going to be fruitful. They are going to multiply, and in this multiplication and fruitfulness, in this dominion that I am giving them, they will have seniority over us."

How can we have seniority over God? Simple. He gives it to us.

In Genesis 1, God excluded himself from the deal he made with mankind when he said, "Let *them* have dominion."

In essence, he was saying: "I have created the heavens for myself, but I put man in charge of the earth."

We must get back to that position of dominion. We must shift out of living according to what men have called us. We must emerge from the veil of religion. We must step into the blessing of God, to where we are wrestling with him and say: "Father, I am not letting you go until you congratulate me."

What is the lesson from this transformative event in Jacob's life? It is that we have to hang on. We have to wrestle God until the sun comes up and declare that we are coming back into our rightful place. So God-bless me, salute me, congratulate me! Amen

WHO ARE YOU?

As Jacob continued to fight God for a blessing, God replied: "What is your name?" In essence, he was asking: "What is the defaming mark of your life?" God brought Jacob back to his name...and then he changed it.

Anytime you are looking for promotion from God, he will first bring you back to your present reality before he promotes you into his reality—the place where his truth and your promotion reside.

God was asking many things of Jacob with: "What is your name?" He was asking Jacob:

What are the defaming marks of your life?

What are the memorials that have been built up in your life?

What are the altars that have been built up in your life?

What are you renowned for?

Well, let's see. Jacob bought some oil and poured it over some rocks, which was not really building an altar. His grandfather was an altar builder. His father was also an altar builder. Jacob had to become an altar builder. He had to be able not only to build for himself but to pull out of what had already been established and build upon—the foundations of past generations, a generational synergy.

Jacob had to answer some tough questions from God. Likewise, each of us, at key moments of our lives, will have to answer the same questions. It's called qualification. It may not feel like it as we are shaking in our boots and wishing we brought a change of pants, but God has a purpose. Look what he did for Job, although the onset of that conversation was anything but comforting.

> *Then the Lord answered Job out of the whirlwind and*
> *said,*
>> *Who is this that darkens counsel*
>> *By words without knowledge?*
>> *Now gird up your loins like a man,*
>> *And I will ask you, and you instruct Me!*
>> *Where were you when I laid the foundation of the earth?*
>
> Job 38:1-4

"Who is this...? What is your name?" Not easy questions, yet once identity is established both for God and the person, we understand the reason for the inquiry: "This is who I am making you. Your new name shall be...."

Jacob was caught between his identity, a rock and who God wanted him to be. I can imagine his response to God's question: "Who are you?"

"I am Jacob. I am a deceiver. I am a supplanter. I am a conman. I am a dysfunctional guy who stole my inheritance from my older brother, Esau. I deceived my father, wound up with a first wife I don't love who is giving me more kids than the second wife who, incidentally, I do love. So, I'm spending more time with the first wife and that is frustrating the second wife. And just when things couldn't get any more messed up, I took the maids of both of them and fathered children with each woman. Later, I had to run from my father-in-law, Laban, who has made cheating me an artform, and now I am running from my brother, Esau, who is seeking revenge. I am Jacob."

Jacob was in a hard place. He had already been to the house of God-Bethel. He had already experienced God on some level, but he was still being pursued. See, when you get to the house of God and experience God there, and those who want to kill you are still in hot pursuit, you have to get beyond the house of God and find God himself at a level that identifies your purpose. In so doing, you just may discover that it was God who orchestrated these events to bring you to the place where you sought him at a greater level—the level he wanted you to reach in him all along.

As we undergo this process, we have to get past who we have been and bring ourselves into a place where we let God deal with us. It is hard to do. This, typically, is not something that counseling or the prayers of others or a good deliverance service can do. Like Jacob, the deep, intransigent things in us must be displaced through wrestling with God one-on-one.

Over the years, I have had to wrestle God. And I have looked over in the corner but there was nobody to tag. That's when I realized that this is not a team match. This is a one-on-one championship bout and God had a better record than I did. But I reached a place where I could tell God: "Congratulate me. I am seeing this thing through."

When the Naphtali stone is in place, we can look in the mirror and see God. We can see his promises being fulfilled. We can hear God saying: "Your name shall no longer be Jacob. Your name shall no longer be deceiver, supplanter. Your name will no longer be conman."

Yes, some of us were adulterers, fornicators, drunkards and thieves, but now we have been changed through the blood of Jesus, and we are promised a new name.

> *He who has an ear, let him hear what the Spirit says to the churches. To him who overcomes, to him I will give some of the hidden manna, and I will give him a white stone, and a new name written on the stone which no one knows but he who receives it.*
>
> Revelation 2:17

"Your name will no longer be Jacob but it will be Israel." This is the manifestation of Naphtali; he is wrestling with God. The name *Israel* means, "God strives." It shows God's faithfulness. There were others in the scripture that carry that name, but *Israel* in the Hebrew comes from the root word *Sarah,* a female name. The root of the

111

name *Jacob*, the father of Naphtali, means "to persist, to preserve, to contend, striving and wrestled (in the past tense)."

FACE TO FACE

Jacob wrestled with God, but God considered himself the loser in that fight even though he won. Why? Because through wrestling, through the Naphtali process, Jacob came into a place where God could congratulate him as a winner, which was God's plan all the time. God could salute Jacob and say: "I am putting you back in charge. I am putting something in you."

Finally, Jacob came to the place in his struggles where he wanted to name the location. He named this place *Peniel*. It means "the face of God, face-to-face."

> So Jacob named the place Peniel, for he said, "I have seen God face to face, yet my life has been preserved."

> Genesis 32:30

Now, face-to-face does not mean Jacob is looking at God nose to nose. Rather, face-to-face means God pulls you alongside him and takes your cheek and puts your cheek to his cheek so that you both are looking in the same direction. How cool is that? You are not merely looking into God's eyes; you are seeing what God sees with his eyes.

When Jacob was at Peniel, he grabbed one of those rocks and he put it under his head. This was a rock from the altar that Abraham had built. Jacob put it under his head and he went to sleep and that's when he saw the heavens open. There was a ladder with angels ascending and descending. They were going up and down, and God spoke to him.

Now, let's understand something here. This was not Jacob's dream; this was God's dream. The dream had been in that rock since Abraham built an altar. And when Jacob laid his head on that rock, some of that dream was shared with him.

So you can meet God in Bethel—the house of God—but to have your name changed and get cheek-to-cheek with God, you have to

112

get with God in Peniel. You have to get face-to-face with God. That is where dreams are birthed. You do not get the dream looking at God in the eye. That is Bethel. You get the dream cheek-to-cheek and seeing what God sees. That is Peniel.

To see where God wants you to go, you have to see what God is seeing. And as you see what God sees, faith fills you. You are encouraged. You are strengthened. You can face the Esau's of your life with courage because you see your challenges through the promises of God. What God promised Abraham and Isaac was now in Jacob because he laid his head on a rock and his whole world changed.

Our world will change as we dream God's dream. We need to explore the Jacob in us and confront him, asking God: "What is your dream for me?"

The dream God reveals will be connected through synergy with the generations of your natural and spiritual family. The things we dream today are not going to be entirely fulfilled. Why? Because we are dreaming partly for the next generation and generations after that.

The dream Jacob received was two generations after Abraham. So, we are never too old. Your grandbabies and your great grandbabies need you to start dreaming God's dream.

Some of us had dreams that were great and then they fell away, crumbled, failed to materialize, and we think God will never do them again. Well, think again:

What are the prophetic words that God spoke over your life?

What are the things that God has said to you?

What are the things that God has poured into you?

What are the things that you dream for but the economy said you could not do it?

Religion said you could not do it.

Your genealogy said you could not do it.

Your standing in society and culture said there was no way that you were going to do it.

Maybe it is your past.

Maybe it is a bad mistake.

Maybe it was a one-night-stand.

Maybe you stole something.

Maybe something happened and you had an accident.

Whatever it may be that is part of your Jacob, you have to come to Peniel and put your head on a rock and let God's dream get into you again. You will prevail and God will congratulate you and say, "Son, well done. I salute you. Now you are back in charge."

Consider Jacob's prayer of thanksgiving to God:

> *Jacob said, "O God of my father Abraham and God of my father Isaac, O Lord, who said to me, 'Return to your country and to your relatives, and I will prosper you, I am unworthy of all the lovingkindness and of all the faithfulness which You have shown to Your servant; for with my staff only I crossed this Jordan, and now I have become two companies.*

Genesis 32: 9-10

He started with nothing but a staff when he crossed the Jordan river, and he wound up prosperous, having more goats, cattle and servants than his father-in-law Laban. God was making him what Abraham had been promised and what Isaac had been promised. Jacob was moving beyond the herder of a bunch of goats, cows, feuding wives and a dozen sons. He was becoming the father of many nations, descendants as numerous as the stars in the sky. The fulfillment was through Jacob but the promise was through Abram when God changed his name just as he changed Jacob's name.

> *No longer shall your name be called Abram,*
> *But your name shall be Abraham;*
> *For I have made you the father of a multitude of nations.*

Genesis 17:5

114

When Abram built the altar, God said: "You are no longer Abram. You are Abraham. You have redeemed the sin of Ham [Noah's son] by building an altar." And in building that altar, Abraham's name was changed.

Jacob laid his head on the broken altar, and God gave him a dream, changed his name and brought him into a place of fulfilling the promise he had made his grandfather Abraham.

CONCLUSION

We need to build an altar today. Some of us need to redeem things through the altar, getting rid of the Jacob in us and having a dream of coming out on the other side, wrestling with God and become Israel.

The process is difficult. Wrestling is never fun. Sometimes my sons say: "Hey Dad, let us wrestle."

Of course, they are grown men now. When they were little, I had to hold back. Today, they could easily kill me. But I don't tell them that. Instead, I say: "Boys, we can't do what we did when you were little. I can't afford to wrestle you."

"What do you mean, Dad? Are you afraid we'll hurt you?"

"No, I'm afraid I'll hurt you. And then I'll have to pay for your doctoring."

When you wrestle with God, you hang on until he is done. It's called paying the price. You hang on until the process is concluded, until Jacob is gone and Israel is living the promise of his grandfather and twelve confederate tribes forming the nation of Israel...all because Jacob was willing to wrestle.

Are you willing? Rachel said, "I have wrestled. This is Naphtali. He is the proof of my wrestling."

Jacob said, "I wrestled. I am Israel now. This is proof of my wrestling with God."

What is your proof that you are wrestling with God today? What is your proof that you are allowing God into the places of your heart that have made you famous?

When you do that, you are able to see Holy Spirit come in a gentle way, so kind, yet so forceful. He is not the one actually struggling. You are the one squirming and weaving and twisting as the name Naphtali says, trying to get out of the grip of God. And God says: "No, you rung the bell. You engaged. You started this fight. We're going to finish it together. Just hang on."

Later, God will say, "Wait a minute. We have been going at it too long. You need to let me go."

But you will say, "No, not until you congratulate me."

Notice, however: The victory was not that Jacob won the match. The victory was the declaration of congratulations from the mouth of God, the *ish*, the spirit man, that was fighting that day. It was God's blessing, released into Jacob's life, that made him the winner. Jacob did not win from the event. He won from the encounter.

You have events at the house of God (Bethel: eye to eye), but you have encounters at the face of God (Peniel: cheek to cheek).

If you want transformation, stop looking for God's eyes and start reaching for his cheek. He wants to pull you up and show you what he sees. "Hey daughter. Hey son. Come on. This is what I see for you and your life. This is what I see for you and your calling and your anointing, the mantle that I have given you."

You may say, "But I am Jacob. I am out of place. I have lost it. I came into great things but I lost them. I had great things but now I have people pursuing me who want to kill me for what I have and how I got it."

But God says, "Wait a minute. Forget the past. Get cheek-to-cheek with me and let us look into the future. Let us press on towards the goal for the prize of the high calling in my son Christ Jesus."

"So Jacob named the place Peniel, for he said, 'I have seen God face-to-face, yet my life has been preserved."

The fight is over. Jacob is finished. His name has been changed. He is no longer a deceiver, supplanter, con man. He lays his head on a rock and he gets a dream. Now he is Israel, and he comes out of this encounter saying: *"I have seen God face-to-face yet my life has been preserved."*

This word *preserved* means "to strip, to deliver oneself, to give oneself over to, to be delivered, to be snatched away, rescued."

So, you may be thinking: *I made it. I am the champion. I have done this. Woo-hoo! Praise God! I have been congratulated by God. I have been saluted by God.* But you come out of wrestling with God and realize you have been stripped and plundered. You thought you won. God changed your name, right? But what God really did was rip out all the old in you and replace it with the new you. That's when you realize that name-change conveys much more than just a new moniker on your mailbox.

Jacob recovered the promise of his grandfather and his father. He was rescued. God wrestled with him to save him, to rescue him from himself, to separate him from the past, to be spared, stripped and delivered...just in time to face his greatest challenge—an angry brother.

> *Then Jacob lifted his eyes and looked, and behold, Esau was coming, and four hundred men with him.*

> Genesis 33:1

Yes, Jacob, now Israel, limped away from his encounter with God, but he was limping in great strength toward victory.

> *Then Esau ran to meet him and embraced him, and fell on his neck and kissed him, and they wept.*

> Genesis 33:4

In 1 Kings 18:21, Elijah asked the children of Israel: *"How long will you hesitate between two opinions?"*

The same word, *hesitate*, is used for *limp*. The root is identical and it means: "Why are you limping here?" Still, the limp of the children of Israel was of a different kind, not of encountering God but of turning away from God.

A wound, in and of itself, is not necessarily good or evil. It depends on who did the wounding and why. Circumcision, as commanded by God to Abraham, is a wound. So is circumcision of the heart. So is the cross of Jesus. God's wounds open us, separate us old from new, bring us into agreement with his heart which also experiences pain. Ultimately, God's wounding brings lifelike freshly planted soil.

> *Faithful are the wounds of a friend,*
> *But deceitful are the kisses of an enemy.*

Proverbs 27:6

God is ready to touch your hip. He is ready to bring you into a place to have yourself, Naphtali, wrestling with him. Yes, we are the incorporated Body of Christ, but you cannot contribute to the corporate until you have wrestled with God personally.

You want a great life? You need to wrestle with God. You have to go through a process. Leave Bethel and get to Peniel and join your face with God's face. Coming to the Father cheek-to-cheek will bring you into that experience of having your name changed, your life changed and the generations changed forever.

You will never be the same again. So let's get ready to rumble!

THE STONE OF GAD

The Harrow

ELIJAH WAS FROM THE TRIBE OF GAD. We understand this from 1 Kings 17:1.

> *Now Elijah the Tishbite, who was of the settlers of Gilead, said to Ahab, "As the LORD, the God of Israel lives, before whom I stand, surely there shall be neither dew nor rain these years, except by my word."*
>
> 1 Kings 17:1

The settlers of Gilead were the tribe of Gad.

The name *Gad* means "a troop cometh or a troop comes." It means "fortune, to cut, to invade, to expose, a harrowing fortune." A *harrow* is a plow. It means "to attack." It describes "making an invasive cut," mostly to expose something that is valuable.

So you see some pattern here: "invasive, invades, runs after, a harrow, digs so it can expose things, cuts the ground so it can expose things that are valuable treasures."

Look at one scripture through two translations.

> *Leah's maid Zilpah bore Jacob a son. Then Leah said, "How fortunate!" So she named him Gad.*
>
> Genesis 30:10-11 NASB [emphasis added]
>
> *And Zilpah Leah's maid bare Jacob a son. And Leah said, A troop cometh: and she called his name Gad.*
>
> Genesis 30:10-11 KJV [emphasis added]

119

Notice that two different phrases are used for the name *Gad*. One is: "how fortunate" and the other is: "a troop cometh." These are really the same phrase and will become important to understand what it means to have Gad's stone in place.

The Hebrew, *begad*, which is the word *gad*, means "fortune." So, how does the King James version get "a troop cometh" out of "fortune"?

First, the King James translators created their version almost 400 years ago, and since that time much more of the Hebrew language has been understood through linguistics and etymology.

Secondly, many translators believe that the word *begad*, (not just *gad* but *begad*) is both an Aramaic word and a Hebrew word. It was originally two words, *bo* and *gad*, combined to form *bogad*, meaning "fortune comes." Leah chose this word, *gad*, for her son because of her good fortune of having been given another son. Now, the word *fortune* is not referring just to money or wealth. Leah meant something different by "her fortune had come."

Gad is also the name of a Babylonian god of fortune. The language of the Babylonians was Aramaic, a sister language to Hebrew. The Hebrew vowel *a* is not pronounced like the *a* in *bad*, but is like the *a* in *father*. Therefore, the Hebrew and the Aramaic word *gad* is pronounced like our English word *god*. It is very likely that our word *god* comes from the Hebrew and the Aramaic word *gad*.

RAIDERS OF GAD

Let us look at Genesis 49:19.

> *As for Gad, raiders shall raid him*
> *But he will raid at their heels.*

In this passage, Israel is giving a prophetic word over Gad. He is saying that raiders will come and take things from Gad, but Gad will chase the raiders and raid them at their heel. I found that in my study of this tribe, the word heel is important in this prophetic name. It gives us an in-depth look at Gad's reaction to the invasion of others into their land intending to rob their inheritance and goods.

We find this word *heel* in several passages throughout the Old Testament, and all with the same meaning.

> *And I will put enmity*
> *Between you and the woman,*
> *And between your seed and her seed;*
> *He shall bruise you on the head,*
> *And you shall bruise him on the heel.*

Genesis 3:15

The word *heel* is the same word that we find in Genesis 49 when referring to the tribe of Gad. It comes from Hebrew culture. When a baby was born, the midwife held it upside down by its ankle and struck the bottom of its foot to get it to take its first breath.

Now, in most modern cultures around the world, we do not slap a baby; they usually start breathing on their own. But in ancient times, they believed that the heel slap called the breath of life to come into the baby. It comes from Genesis where God put his nostrils to man's nostrils and breathed into Adam. From that point on, they believed that by tapping or slapping the heel that the breath of God came into the baby and therefore drew its first breath of life.

God was telling the serpent in Genesis 3: "When the Son of Man (or Son of God) comes into the world, you will bruise him to the point of taking his life, but God, who is the resurrection and the life, will raise him from the dead and he will destroy your authority on the earth."

The same thing is being expressed by God in Genesis 49:19. "Raiders will come after Gad but Gad will pursue them to the point of taking their life from them. He will pursue them on their heel, sticking their heel until there is no more life left in them. He will crush your head."

INVADERS

In the natural, Gad tended to let others live alongside him in his land. Nothing wrong with that on the surface. We're supposed to share, right? Not always. Some things are sacred. Sometimes sharing leads to an invasion.

One of the downfalls of having the stone of Gad out of place is that we attempt to coexist with everyone around us, not just in the natural but also spiritually. Often, we end up allowing darkness to envelop us. We permit things in our communities and cultures that are contrary to the Kingdom of God. When there are things around us that are contrary to the Kingdom of God, we need to cut them off and not allow them in our land.

You may say, "Well, aren't we supposed to all get along?" No, Jesus never told us to get along. He told us—the Ekklesia—to take over. Now, that doesn't mean we are to not love people, but we are to be the standard-setters in culture. That is who we are. Instead, we have allowed an ungodly discipling of our culture in the past several decades that has created an entirely new culture, one in direct opposition to God on many fronts.

Like Gad, we have been invaded and our inheritance is being stolen. Our lands have been taken. Our government has been occupied. Our positions of influence have been compromised. Our voices are being muted. God is telling us that we must put the Gad stone back in place. We must pursue our enemies and cut them off at the very root. We must strike them at the heel in a way that they lose their voice, their influence and their grip on our inheritance.

This is what it will take to bring about awakening and revival in the nations of our world. If we do not act, indeed, if we lay passive while continuing to coexist with ungodly lifestyles and choices; if we try to be a religion instead of a kingdom, we will never achieve the will of the Father's heart on the earth. We must shift out of coexisting and into a place of reigning.

COMPLACENCY

Now, the tribe of Gad could be a rough bunch but they were also vulnerable and complacent in allowing their homes to be invaded. They thought there was no danger in merely sharing. People of other cultures passing through their borders as they please and intermingling with their families presented no discernible danger...until they ran off with Gad's possessions.

That is where we are today as the church. We allow a lot of intermingling and suddenly realize we have lost our nation. We have lost our regions. We have lost our cities. We have lost our hope. A great number of our churches in America, not all, are nothing more than a gathering to sing a few songs and listen to some rooster strutting across the platform preaching moral platitudes and personal validation. And we think we are okay.

> *There is a way which seems right to a man*
> *But its end is the way of death.*

Proverbs 16:25

We will not be okay until we get back to being Holy Spirit led, serving God with all our beings. We might preach some things that offend people, but if it brings about the truth and righteousness of God, it's worth it. We have got to shift from entertaining people to empowering, commissioning, releasing and launching people into their places of influence for the Kingdom of God.

The tribe of Gad didn't make this distinction. They were complacent, and that made them vulnerable to the destructive effects of intermingling with ungodly cultures. Consequently, the raiders of Genesis 49 stole their source of life. Coexistence with the enemy will rob us of life. You may say, "Well, we need to influence them. We need to convert them into the Kingdom of God." To a certain extent, yes. The key, however, is to be among them without becoming a part of them—in their world but not of their world.

> *I do not ask You to take them out of the world, but to*
> *keep them from the evil one. They are not of the world,*

> *even as I am not of the world. Sanctify them in the truth;*
> *Your word is truth.*

John 17:15-17

There is a movement in the modern church that says to win people, we must be like them. So, we have smoke machines and torn jeans and compromising preaching. We have light shows, drama, theater, rock concert music...anything to draw people into the church for sixty minutes and make them comfortably entertained enough to return the following week.

But that is not what God told us to use. Jesus told us in John 17. "Your word is truth." The word of God in power will attract people. It will also get them born-again.

We have something in us, a part of us that is greater than any of those surface attractions. We have Holy Spirit. He is the power of God. The Bible says that signs and wonders and miracles are for the unbeliever, not light shows and skinny jeans. (Although getting me into a pair of skinny jeans would be miracle enough. LOL!) God has given us signs, wonders and miracles to bring the lost into the Kingdom of God, not to fill our churches but to activate them by moving people into becoming who God created them to be sons and daughters.

RIVERS IN THE DESERT

As we said earlier, Gad's name also means "fortune." This is an interesting word. On the surface, it means to make one rich or discover a treasure. But here's the meaning of *fortune* in Gad's name: "a cutting harrow." Now, a harrow is a plow, and that plow is connected to other harrows, and they dig into the ground. Its purpose is to turn over the soil, kicking out the rocks and exposing the nutrients of the soil hidden just below the surface. So, when you plant your seeds in freshly plowed soil, those seeds can have access to nutritious soil.

The word *fortune* also means "to cut as a river through a desert or through a landscape in the sense of disturbing topography." The prophetic picture here is of a great river pouring forcefully and violently into a desert. And it is coming from where? From the throne of God. The Bible tells us:

> *Then [the angel] showed me a river of the water of life, clear as crystal, coming from the throne of God and of the Lamb...*

Revelation 22:1

That river is on its way, coming strongly and violently, hitting this desert place like a plow churning out soil and exposing treasures. This river digs its own channel in the desert.

There are people in the church today who do not want to go into the desert places. They prefer the air-conditioned building and padded pew, hearing how they can make their lives better until next Sunday when they are wrecked again. This is not who God is looking for.

God is looking for an Ekklesia—sons and daughters with a mantle of Gad upon them to go into dry places with the river of God pouring out of them, bringing life to dry and dusty places where no life is growing at all. God is calling us to this. Hallelujah!

> *Behold, I will do something new,*
> *Now it will spring forth;*
> *Will you not be aware of it?*
> *I will even make a roadway in the wilderness,*
> *Rivers in the desert.*

Isaiah 43:19

In Ezekiel, God took the prophet into a valley full of dry bones and asked him a question.

> *He asked me, "Son of man, can these bones live?" I said, "Sovereign LORD, you alone know."*
> *Then he said to me, "Prophesy to these bones"*

Ezekiel 37:3-4

Ezekiel answered wisely, right? In response, God gave him a list of things to prophesy. Ezekiel had to participate with God to get that exceedingly great army standing upright and ready for battle. God

125

had a passion and a purpose in his heart, but he took the man of God and sent him to a valley full of dead dry bones to call to life.

God is going to pick us up and put us in some places that are dry and dead so life can come and armies can begin to rise up. But here's the key. We must overcome the death and dryness and not let it overcome us! To do so, we must be prepared. We must be called and ready for the challenges.

We are headed into every sphere of society. This is not just for the church or revival for a bunch of staid Christians. This is to awaken the nations to God so that their hearts turn back to him. God is challenging us. God is shifting us into desert places.

A voice of one calling:
"In the wilderness prepare
the way for the Lord;
make straight in the desert
a highway for our God."

Isaiah 40:3

This passage really knocks a hole in the notion that God is going to do everything sovereignly, right? God is not doing everything on the earth sovereignly. If God is going to do something on the earth, he needs a man or woman to do it. That is why Jesus came as a man, not as God, to bring order out of disorder. As God brings revival and awakening, he is enacting transformation and reformation. Yet he is going to need a remnant to carry it out—a group of people to rise up and say as the prophet said, "Here I am. Send me."

"Prepare the way..." for whom? The Lord, the owner. Where? In the wilderness—outside our comfort zones, beyond our safe places where the balmy breeze is always blowing. We are making straight in the desert, a highway for our God. Why does God need a highway? It means a place where God can move freely through these places and bring life to its inhabitants.

Thus says the Lord,
Who makes a way through the sea
And a path through the mighty waters,

Who brings forth the chariot and the horse,
The army and the mighty man
(They will lie down together and not rise again;
They have been quenched and extinguished like a wick):
"Do not call to mind the former things,
Or ponder things of the past.
"Behold, I will do something new,
Now it will spring forth;
Will you not be aware of it?
I will even make a roadway in the wilderness,
Rivers in the desert.
"The beasts of the field will glorify Me,
The jackals and the ostriches,
Because I have given waters in the wilderness
And rivers in the desert,
To give drink to My chosen people.

Isaiah 43:16-20

God is bringing us into a new place, although it is not something that is coming. It is here now, and it is like nothing that has come before it. We have to learn how to steward the revival and reformation that this new move of God is igniting. Casual encounters with the power of God will not get it done. God is moving us from encounters to stewardship of what he brings to us.

Listen to me, you who pursue righteousness,
Who seek the Lord:
Look to the rock from which you were hewn
And to the quarry from which you were dug.
Look to Abraham your father
And to Sarah who gave birth to you in pain;
When he was but one I called him,
Then I blessed him and multiplied him."
Indeed, the Lord will comfort Zion;
He will comfort all her waste places.
And her wilderness He will make like Eden,

And her desert like the garden of the Lord;
Joy and gladness will be found in her,
Thanksgiving and sound of a melody.

Isaiah 51:1-3

We are cut from kingdom cloth. We are hewn from the kingdom rock—Jesus Christ himself, our elder brother.

FALSE CROWNS

Mankind was created to thrive in the presence of God, and God is bringing us back to that place where we are not just visiting his presence once in a while but are actually living and working from his presence—his Eden.

As we do this, right here on earth, we will reign in life. We will see nations changed. Individuals and people groups will surrender to the King of Kings and the Lord of Lords, not for a trip to heaven but for the activation of their purpose in God's plan and will for the earth. It won't always be easy or pretty. At times, it will be rough. Look what Moses said prophetically about Gad:

Of Gad he said,
"Blessed is the one who enlarges Gad;
He lies down as a lion,
And tears the arm, also the crown of the head.
"Then he provided the first part for himself,
For there the ruler's portion was reserved;
And he came with the leaders of the people;
He executed the justice of the Lord,
And His ordinances with Israel."

Deuteronomy 33:20-21

God is stirring an anointing in us today to get the Gad stone back in place where we rip false crowns off of things that have set up their thrones in our nation, communities, families and churches.

There are false crowns of sickness, diseases and pandemics trying to take over society. Yet it is not just the diseases themselves. The threat of them is being used by wicked people to promote an evil agenda. They shut down businesses, schools, churches, even entire economies for their political purposes. There is a false crown of abortion masquerading as the right to choose. There are false crowns everywhere that people are too fearful or too blinded to pull off.

In this passage, there is a portion for the King that was reserved. This represents the Ekklesia in that culture. They executed the justice of the Lord and his ordinances with Israel. They helped hold Israel accountable to the ordinance of God, the ways of God and the standards of God.

We need that in the church today. There are things running rampant that are hindering us, making us weak and ineffective among the nations.

God never intended the church to be a secluded group of individuals. God has called us to be a remnant that stands and holds each other accountable. There is an accountability that is being released in the house of God. The Bible says that judgment starts at the house of God, not for condemnation but for restoration and reactivation into who God's called us to be in executing his will on the earth.

When the stone of Gad is out of place, we find ourselves in a narrow place. Instead of a troop of liberation, we become an enslaved people. There is no fortune, no digging of treasure. We are continually invaded and overtaken with no ability to pursue those who have stolen our inheritances and diverted our purposes. The place we inhabit is dry, dead and religious. There is no water of Holy Spirit cutting through the dry places, no revival, no awakening, no reformation and no transformation happening in our nations. The enemy continues to occupy our land and wreak havoc in our culture.

When Gad's stone is back in place, everything begins to change. *"Blessed is the one who enlarges Gad."* We have to enlarge Gad by getting that stone back in place. These attributes of this anointing of Gad bring the fire of God, but not for one dramatic event. The fire of

129

God is to turn the hearts of the people back to Him, to live continually before him.

JUSTICE

> *[Gad] executed the justice of the Lord,*
> *And His ordinances with Israel.*

This "justice" is not the so-called social justice of today where certain people groups who feel they have been treated unfairly expect to rise to power, destroy our cultures and weaken our nations through the enemy's agenda. Let us say: "Hell no to that! We will not allow it."

We are to execute judgment. We are not to coexist with evil in any of its forms but to stand and be the Ekklesia at the gate which determines what can and cannot come into our nation. This is about the will and heart of God.

We have turned from preachers of the gospel to politicians of the people. Why are we not preaching on abortion more? Why are we not preaching against same-sex marriage? Why are we not speaking up about transgenders and cross-dressers indoctrinating our children in elementary school? Why are we not teaching the people that certain things are wrong and are bringing destruction to the nation instead of God's blessings? We must confront this non-kingdom culture that is forcefully invading our nations and trying to change us to be like them. We must awaken kingdom culture!

We avoid these touchy issues to keep butts in seats, budgets met and buildings full. We operate in the spirit of a politician. We have to get out of that. We have to stand and get on the heel of these things, breaking the life out of them so they have no ability to influence, change or to even agitate our culture.

Kingdom culture brings a justice that promotes the will and intent of God's heart. When the Gad stone is in place, heaven and earth come into alignment and power is returned to its rightful owners—the Ekklesia of God, the sons and the daughters of God. That is true justice.

GAD IN PLACE

What happens when we get the stone in place? We find ourselves in a large place, ever-expanding and growing the territory that God has given us individually and corporately. We become a truth that pursues the enemy when he has come after our inheritance and purpose. We get our goods back and activate our inheritance to fulfill the will of God. Our fortune is unearthed and treasures—gifts and precious things from the heart of the Father—are no longer hidden but manifested in our lives.

We have to activate these things again in the church. We need people baptized in the Holy Spirit, speaking in tongues, activating the gifts of Jesus—the apostles, prophets, evangelists, pastors and teachers.

When the stone is back in place, we are no longer dry, dusty, dead religious people. We occupy once again the places in culture that the Father meant for us to occupy from the beginning of time. We become a people of kingdom government and rulership, distributing the good news of our King. Our sonship is restored and we move forward in life through partnership with God, doing his will on the earth, not ours.

Our purpose is not about ourselves. It is about God's heart-desire being manifested on the earth. We do not belong to ourselves anymore. We belong to God when we are born again. Paul said:

> *I have been crucified with Christ; and it is no longer I who live, but Christ lives in me; and the life which I now live in the flesh I live by faith in the Son of God, who loved me and gave Himself up for me.*

Galatians 2:20

> *Even so consider yourselves to be dead to sin, but alive to God in Christ Jesus.*

Romans 6:11

When the Gad stone is in place, we experience the cutting of a new river through the deserts of our life and culture—mighty rivers of the Holy Spirit invading nations and causing the revival, awakening, reformation and transformation of the nations into what Father has in his heart and mind. We are in a mighty invasion of the river of God on the earth.

CONCLUSION

How will all this happen? I am glad you asked. It will happen when the stone of Gad is back into its place and the sons and daughters of the kingdom birth a Holy Spirit invasion that plows into the deserts of our nations, creating new river channels of God's flow, bringing this new life into desert places.

> *He who believes in Me, as the Scripture said, 'From his innermost being will flow rivers of living water.'" But this He spoke of the Spirit, whom those who believed in Him were to receive; for the Spirit was not yet given, because Jesus was not yet glorified.*

> John 7:38-39

From our innermost beings, a mighty river of living water will flow. Not a peaceful little stream. This is not the daisy-in-the-hair Jesus movement of the '60s. This is a violent river gushing out of us, changing the landscape wherever it flows.

Are you ready? I am ready. God is ready. The nations are ready. They are crying out for it. The earth is groaning for it.

> *For the creation was subjected to futility, not willingly, but because of Him who subjected it.*

> Romans 8:20

> *Jesus answered and said to her, "If you knew the gift of God, and who it is who says to you, 'Give Me a drink,' you would have asked Him, and He would have given you living water."*

> John 4:10

We know the gift of God, and we know who is speaking to us. The Lion of Judah is getting ready to roar because of who is in us.

Out of our innermost being, this river is flowing. Not out of our gifts, talents, anointing, calling, title or education. It is flowing out of Him.

> *It is the Spirit who gives life; the flesh profits nothing; the words that I have spoken to you are spirit and are life.*

John 6:63

When the stone of Gad is in place, the river of Holy Spirit flows. There is an invasion of Holy Spirit coming into the earth like we have never seen. We must ready ourselves by getting the Gad stone back in place.

If we are going to see an outpouring in the nations, it is not going to be a denomination that does it. It is going to be the Spirit of God destroying the works of the enemy in our land and turning deserts to places where everything under God's heaven can flourish.

The Stone of Asher

Righteousness

ASHER WAS THE FAVORITE AMONG HIS BROTHERS, and God's great blessing was upon him. God made Asher some incredible promises. Despite this favor, however, we do not see much written about Asher in scripture.

As with all the tribes, there were things that happened when the stone was out of place or when Asher was not living up to his name. These were times when the blessing of the Lord is not realized.

For example, Asher did not run some of the giants out of his land. Instead, he allowed them to dwell with him there. Yet God loved Asher and wanted him fruitful, protected, rich and blessed for generations.

Let's look at the tribe of Asher from two different translations of Moses' blessing in Deuteronomy.

First, the New American Standard Bible:

> *More blessed than sons is Asher;*
> *May he be favored by his brothers,*
> *And may he dip his foot in oil.*
> *Your locks will be iron and bronze,*
> *And according to your days,*
> *So will your leisurely walk be.*

Deuteronomy 33:24-25

And from the Contemporary English Version:

The Lord's greatest blessing
is for you, tribe of Asher.
You will be the favorite
of all the other tribes.
You will be rich with olive oil
and have strong town gates
with bronze and iron bolts.
Your people will be powerful
for as long as they live.

Deuteronomy 33:24-25 CEV

In these passages, God is giving a blessing into the tribe of Asher for generations to come, and in so doing, telling us about him. Asher's people will be powerful. The enemy will not be able to penetrate Asher's cities, and the city gates will be spectacular like no other city gates. They will be made from things that other cities cannot afford. And there will be no breaking of the gates. They will not break under pressure nor give way when the enemy tries to ramrod them.

The name *Asher* means several things, among them: "right (or upright), to reprove, establish, prosperity not due to a curious coincidence but to an obvious correlation of <u>righteousness</u> and <u>efficiency</u>."

EFFICIENCY

That word *efficiency* is important. It means: "order, planning, logistical, productive."

When Asher's stone is in place, there is order and predictable results. We have what we need when we need it. We rely not on serendipitous events for our lives but on the sustained fruits of righteousness.

With Asher's stone in place, there is much help for our journey. We are a blessed, happy, full of joy. We live out of the gift of righteousness and right relationship with the Father. There is a shifting into kingship and kingly anointing outside the bounds of condemnation and frustration. There is a flow of power and blessing and an order in lives and nations. There is the hitting of the mark like an arrow shot from a seasoned marksman's bow. There is purpose to discover and will to be obeyed, and a destiny to be walked out.

When Asher's stone is out of place, this scripture goes unfulfilled:

> *He who began a good work in you will perfect it*
> *until the day of Christ Jesus.*

Philippians 1:6

Our paths become clogged with things that hinder our walk with the Father. We miss the destiny that God has ordained for us.

When Asher's stone is out of place, there is no help for our journey. There is only sadness, misery, brokenness; we are busted and disgusted. We rely on coincidence or happenstance to get blessings into our lives. There is condemnation, no order in life, nothing moves logistically. Chaos is everywhere as we see in the nations today. There is no production, no performance of the will of the Father. There is unrighteousness and evil motives, and the life God intended for us never materializes.

RIGHTEOUSNESS

Asher's tribe is most associated with righteousness. The word *righteous* is the Greek word *dikaios*, meaning "justice, correct righteousness, innocent, right or right relationship."

This is why we care about the tribe of Asher today. These are characteristics we must bring into our lives and nations as God shifts us back to a place of living righteously. When we look at our nation, we see similar things to what scriptures spoke of thousands of years ago:

> *There is a kind [of person] who is pure in his own eyes,*
> *Yet is not washed from his filthiness.*

Proverbs 30:12

In those days there was no king in Israel; everyone did what was right in his own eyes.

Judges 21:25

Today, we have people doing their own thing. To be accepted in society, political correctness must be adhered to in America, Australia and throughout the world. The mobs of social enforcers require us to approve of the ungodliness in the world. If we don't, we are not considered Christian because modern Christianity says we must love everybody—not only love them but love their way of life and approve of it publicly.

Yet the Bible says we do not love sin; we love the sinner. To love people, we do not have to agree with their iniquities and blatant defilement of God. We love them in the belief that God wants to redeem them—to save them from their sin.

Asher's stone is out of place in the nation today. Unrighteousness is prevailing; it has gained a foothold in our nation. As a result, God wants his Ekklesia, as his legislative arm of heaven, to shift the nation back into its righteous position with heaven and the Father. The importance of this cannot be understated.

Blessed are those who hunger and thirst for righteousness, for they shall be satisfied.

Matthew 5:6

The *righteousness* we hunger and thirst for means "justice, correct, righteous, innocence, right relationship with God."

Notice the passion in the phrase "hunger and thirst." We will be filled from the passion of our hearts, not the condemnation of the unrighteous. This describes an ardent desire for right relationship with God because of who he is—merciful, loving, slow to anger, desiring to bless. He is a good Father. He has positioned us to cry "Abba Father!" Not out of desperation or our own merit but out of love, passion, thanksgiving and gratefulness of heart for what he has done for us. *Only* because of his grace!

138

> *Amazing Grace*
> *how sweet the sound*
> *that saved a wretch like me.*
> *I once was lost*
> *but now am found*
> *was blind but now I see.*

John Newton, 1772

God has brought us out of darkness and into the light. He placed us in right relationship with him as described by the qualities of Asher, all because we yearned for it but had no clue how to obtain it.

In answer to our hearts, God brings us deeper into Holy Spirit, closer to him. He teaches us his ways. We want to live for him because of his love that he pours on us. This is the work of righteousness in our lives. This is the Asher stone in place. It brings righteousness.

Righteousness is a powerful thing and it carries consequences—some pleasant and some not so pleasant. Jesus foretold this in Matthew.

> *Blessed are those who have been <u>persecuted</u> for*
> *the sake of righteousness, for theirs is the kingdom*
> *of heaven.*

Matthew 5:10 [emphasis added]

True righteousness could result in persecution. Of course, many people are persecuted because of their religious ways. When different religious sects fight, there is persecution of one group or another. However, this scripture refers to being persecuted because of a right relationship with God.

How do we handle persecution? We take a stand and keep on standing. True righteousness says:

- We have received that gift of righteousness.
- We have right relationship with God.
- We will not compromise God.

- We will not shun him for the things that others are doing.
- We will not compromise our righteousness to be politically correct.
- We will not compromise righteousness so people in the world accept us.
- We stand firm in our right relationship with God.

It was by God's grace and love that we were brought into this righteous relationship. Not by our works or deeds but by the death, burial, resurrection, ascension and enthronement of Jesus at the right hand of the Father.

UNRIGHTEOUSNESS

The unrighteous have gained political power in our nation and they are influencing decisions. The Bible tells us:

> *When the righteous increase, the people rejoice,*
> *But when a wicked man rules, people groan.*

Proverbs 29:2

There is a lot of groaning in the world. It is the result of unrighteousness. Yet the media says everything's fine. Certain politicians and people groups praise the destruction of godly order. Riots in the streets are encouraged. Looting stores and burning buildings are just reparations for systemic oppression. Large gatherings of people are fine as long as they're protesting and not worshiping God. Why? Because a core group of people, inspired by the devil, wants to remove God from every aspect of life.

And it's not just because they hate God. It is because the devil is afraid of us. He is afraid of born-again believers who are in right relationship with God. This is because he knows that Jesus' death and resurrection bring us into a place of authority, empowerment and kingdom advancement. (Funny how the devil often has more revelation about Christians than Christians do. Well...maybe not so funny.)

The authority in our lives enables us to tear down every high place that the devil has built in the nations. Therefore, we are to pull down every false idol and every false god. We are to put our foot on the neck of serpents and scorpions and every enemy that has come against the Kingdom of God. We are to bring light to darkness.

LOSING OUR RELIGION

The enemy wants to hinder us from being the Christ-like son or daughter that God made us through the gift of righteousness. Interestingly, the devil does not mind us being religious, but he hates the Ekklesia.

Jesus understood the distinction between religion and right relationship with God when he told the people:

> For I say to you that unless your righteousness surpasses that of the scribes and Pharisees, you will not enter the kingdom of heaven.

Matthew 5:20

The religious leaders of Judaism of that day gave Jesus hell. They actually crucified him not because he was a man of crime or sin or blasphemy but because he was wrecking their religious establishment. And indeed, he was.

Jesus used a parable to put it to them plainly.

> But no one puts a patch of unshrunk cloth on an old garment; for the patch pulls away from the garment, and a worse tear results. Nor do people put new wine into old wineskins; otherwise the wineskins burst, and the wine pours out and the wineskins are ruined; but they put new wine into fresh wineskins, and both are preserved.

Matthew 9:16-17

Jesus was telling the religious leaders: "I have not come to fix your dead, old religion. I have come to tear down that temple of religious posturing and raise up a new one, a living one, a relationship with the Father based on the righteousness that I will provide."

> *Jesus answered them, "Destroy this temple, and in three days I will raise it up." The Jews then said, "It took forty-six years to build this temple, and will You raise it up in three days?"*

John 2:19-20

Of course, he was speaking about his resurrection, a blessing that everyone, including the religious leaders, could have had through him. Yet they rejected him and all he offered. The Pharisees and the scribes wanted to earn righteousness through their deeds, public praying, fasting and religious traditions. They cared more about pleasing men than pleasing God.

Today, we can have all the religious traditions we want, but they will never produce right relationship with God. Why? Because we can't earn it. We can only receive it, and that by making it our first priority.

> *But seek first His kingdom and His righteousness, and all these things will be added to you.*

Matthew 6:33

Now, *to seek* does not mean to look for the kingdom as if it is hiding, but to explore the depths, to submerge into the kingdom. It described a lifetime pursuit as our priority.

THE KINGDOM OF RIGHT RELATIONSHIP

In Matthew 6, Jesus tells us to seek two things: God's kingdom and his righteousness.

The word *kingdom* is made up of two words, *king* and *domain*. So, the kingdom is the King's domain. Yet Jesus is also telling us that we cannot see the kingdom outside of right relationship with God.

This is why Jesus told Nicodemus (a Jewish priest who came to Jesus in the middle of the night) that "unless one is born again, he cannot see the Kingdom of God."

Notice what Jesus didn't say. He didn't say: "Unless one is born again, *he cannot go to heaven.*" But that is what religion

142

teaches—Jesus as a ticket to heaven. Instead, Jesus was saying: "Unless you are born again, you cannot *see* or *participate* in the King's dominion."

Having the stone of Asher in place positions us for kingly dominion through Holy Spirit. Here's what it looks like:

> And [Holy Spirit], when He comes, will convict the world concerning sin and righteousness and judgment; concerning sin, because they do not believe in Me; and concerning righteousness, because I go to the Father and you no longer see Me; and concerning judgment, because the ruler of this world has been judged.
>
> John 16:8-11

This word *convict* used in this passage is the word *reprove*, one of the meanings of Asher's name. *Reprove* means "to establish," another quality of having the stone of Asher in place. Jesus was saying that when Holy Spirit comes, he will establish us.

Now, *the world* in this passage is not earth. It is not even humans. It is the systems *of* this world. Jesus is reaching the world's systems through the Ekklesia by sending us into them with his agenda to convict the world of sin and establish us in righteousness and judgment.

This understanding shocks religious people. Religion tells us the earth belongs to the devil, that he is the prince of the world. Well, not no more. Jesus is the authority on earth. Matthew 28:18 says:

> And Jesus came up and spoke to them, saying, "All authority has been given to Me in heaven and on earth."

With his authority, Jesus is dispatching us. We are taking territory! Jesus establishes us in righteousness because he goes to the Father. The Holy Spirit establishes, convicts, reproves and establishes us in right relationship because Jesus has restored order.

Another meaning of *Asher* is "order." He brings things in order. Heaven's order is that Holy Spirit dwells in us.

Religion has brought us into a place so dysfunctional that even though we have Holy Spirit within us, we still think we can work our way into righteousness. Yet scripture is clear:

> Just as David also speaks of the blessing on the man to whom God credits righteousness <u>apart from works.</u>

Romans 4:6 [emphasis added]

Works has nothing to do with righteousness. You cannot work your way into righteousness; it is a free gift to all who receive it.

> For if by the transgression of the one, death reigned through the one, much more those who receive the abundance of grace and of the gift of righteousness will reign in life through the One, Jesus Christ.

Romans 5:17

This is speaking of Adam as the transgressor, and it shows us how to flow in the royalty of our lives. Through Adam, death reigned, death was in charge. But through Jesus' death and resurrection, life reigns. When? Now. Not in the future. Now. Not after some rapture snatches us out of the earth. Now. It is available to us through righteousness...Now.

Yet we must receive this gift of righteousness. We must get a grip on it, be married to it, occupy it, let it take over and seize upon this abundance of grace. It will shift us into royalty and make us the kings that God has called us to be.

Grace is unmerited favor, but what does that mean? *Favor* means God opens doors for us that no one else can open and closes doors that no one else can close. He brings us into alignment and order—the order of the Asher stone. Grace is God's ability to do in us what we cannot do ourselves.

RIGHTEOUSNESS AS WARFARE

God has dreams, vision and purpose for his Ekklesia, and he wants it to function as originally intended. Jesus came to restore that function.

We were created to inhabit Eden. *Eden* means "the presence of God, the atmosphere of God's presence." Adam and Even fell out of that, but God, through Jesus, restored our relationship with him so we can inhabit his presence and do the things that Jesus did.

Now, that sounds strange to some people. The world and religion say: "You can't be Jesus." Yet Jesus says:

> *Truly, truly, I say to you, he who believes in Me, the works that I do, he will do also; and greater works than these he will do; because I go to the Father.*

John 14:12

> *Behold, I have given you authority to tread on serpents and scorpions, and over all the power of the enemy, and nothing will injure you.*

Luke 10:19

So, we have the authority to do greater works than Jesus? Of course we do! He said so! All has been restored to God's original intent to reign through Jesus Christ. The Greek word for *reign* is *Basileou* meaning "to be king and reign as King."

When the stone of Asher is out of place, we lose that kingly anointing and operate in a peasant or servant mindset. But when the Asher stone is in place, we walk as kings under the King and Lord.

As Asher's stone is repaired, cleansed, healed, washed and put back in its place, we are going to see the fire of God fall. We understand how we reign in life. Not the afterlife, but in the now-life. And in this reign, we war with the weapon of righteousness, the power of God and his truth.

In the word of truth, in the power of God; by the weapons of righteousness for the right hand and the left.

2 Corinthians 6:7

Greater is He who is in you than he who is in the world.

1 John 4:4

Righteousness is not sinlessness in the sense that we are perfect. It is sinlessness in that God has redeemed us from sins and empowered us to walk as he walked on the earth as kings and priests. Righteousness is a weapon, and those who receive it are born again.

If you know that He is righteous, you know that everyone also who practices righteousness is born of Him.

1 John 2:29

Jesus, in right relationship with the Father, judges and wages war. He is our example.

And I saw heaven opened, and behold, a white horse, and He who sat on it is called Faithful and True, and in righteousness He judges and wages war.

Revelation 19:11

Righteousness empowers us to release righteous judgments and fight righteous wars. However, there is a catch. When we war in the spirit, we do not go as foot soldiers. We battle as kings with the help of angel-armies to accomplish the assignments of God. Our right relationship with God is the empowerment in our lives. That is what it means to put the Asher stone back in place.

And Pagiel the son of Ochran over the tribal army of the sons of Asher.

Numbers 10:26

HUMBLE AND HAPPY

Asher was a tribal army known for fighting hard. Interestingly, however, another meaning of Asher's name is "happy."

Then Leah said, "Happy am I! For women will call me happy." So she named him Asher.

Genesis 30:13

So, the tribe of Asher kicked butt with smiles on their faces. Hallelujah! They could come together with other tribes and defeat their enemies and then celebrate with a feast!

As for Asher, his food shall be rich
And he will yield royal dainties.

Genesis 49:20

Despite their prowess on the battlefield, when Asher's stone is in place, there is no room for pride, arrogance or foolishness. There is only a humbleness to come before the Lord.

Nevertheless some men of Asher, Manasseh and Zebulun humbled themselves and came to Jerusalem.

2 Chronicles 30:11

In this particular passage, they were invited to Jerusalem for Passover and they humbled himself. Some of the tribes would not do that but Asher did and God blessed them. As James tells us:

God is opposed to the proud, but gives grace to the humble.

James 4:6

Humility is knowing that you cannot do what you do without God and that anything you do is because God is doing it with you through right relationship.

CONCLUSION

Be encouraged. Asher's stone is being systematically healed and placed in our lives and in the nations. Righteousness is being established so that the fire of God can fall and bring the awakening that we have been seeking. It is coming. It is here. We have crossed the threshold.

> *"For I know the plans that I have for you," declares the Lord, "plans for welfare and not for calamity to give you a future and a hope."*

Jeremiah 29:11

God has positioned us in a place of all spiritual blessings in heavenly places in Christ Jesus.

> *Blessed be the God and Father of our Lord Jesus Christ, who has blessed us with every spiritual blessing in the heavenly places in Christ,*

Ephesians 1:3

As we step into our identity and calling and walk out the assignment God gave us, we are bringing nations into alignment with God's plan. Today, nations are coming into alignment with God. We have stepped into awakening and revival and the outpouring of the fire of God. The kingdoms of this world are becoming the kingdoms of our God in every gate of society.

We will see the power and glory of God coming to the earth.

THE STONE OF ISSACHAR

Knowledge

THE SCRIPTURE BELOW GIVES US INSIGHT into the characteristics of the Issachar tribe, the role that they played and how they contributed to the overall health, progression and safety of the nation of Israel. They understood the times and knew what the nation should do. They were the answer people.

> *Of the sons of Issachar, men who understood the times, with knowledge of what Israel should do, their chiefs were two hundred; and all their kinsmen were at their command.*

1 Chronicles 12:32

In Hebrew, *Issachar* means: "a recompense, to return in kind, to give for something, giving payment, to receive something to give and receive, to understand the times with knowledge, wisdom, prophetic insight." They were a prophetic tribe.

When the stone of Issachar is healed and put back into its place, we will see healing come to the nations.

There has never been a time like today, one in which the church, for the most part, does not know what to do. People in America and abroad frequently ask me: "What is God saying? What should we be doing? What should we believe? What should we be rejecting?"

Yes, those who came before us struggled with some of the same things, but we are faced with issues today that the church has never before faced on this level and magnitude. If we can get the stone of Issachar back in place, if we can bring healing and repair to the altar of God so the fire of God would fall, we will see healing brought to the world because we will know what to do.

MOVE FORWARD

When you don't know what to do, fear sets in, people stay still, chaos erupts, the enemy invades and his agenda takes root. We are seeing the majority of the church doing that today.

Yet God wants his church in motion. We are not called to be stagnant. We are not retreating. We are moving forward. We are pressing on towards the mark of the prize of the high calling that is in Christ Jesus.

> Brethren, I do not regard myself as having laid hold of it yet; but one thing I do: forgetting what lies behind and reaching forward to what lies ahead, I press on toward the goal for the prize of the upward call of God in Christ Jesus. Let us therefore, as many as are perfect, have this attitude; and if in anything you have a different attitude, God will reveal that also to you; however, let us keep living by that same standard to which we have attained.

Philippians 3:13-16

We need the Issachar anointing flowing in the church today. It is vital to seeing and receiving the fire of God into our lives and nations. This is not about individuals' relationships with God, but about the Ekklesia—the body of Christ coming together to bring the awakening and revival that we need and have been crying out for.

The fact is, God is waiting on us, the church; we are not waiting on God. We need to rise up in the prophetic function and apostolic anointing that God has given his Ekklesia. We need the Issachar stone in place so we will know what to do. We don't need any more *good* ideas. We need *God* ideas. We do not need to hear from man.

We need to hear from God. We need to hear from God through his sons and daughters. Then we will have answers as never before.

THE TIMES WE LIVE IN

If there has ever been a day when we need to walk in the Spirit, it is today, so our nation can navigate through these turbulent times.

> *Why are the nations in an uproar and the people devising a vain thing?*

> Psalm 2:1

This verse asks questions of us today, questions that demand answers.

- Why are the nations of the world in an uproar?
- Why are we seeing things today on an unprecedented scale that we have never seen before?

In times past, we saw protests which were largely peaceful. Today we are seeing organized riots and looting. Groups are actually bringing death and anarchy in our nation, defying the laws of the nation and defying God. Never before in the history of America— this great nation that God birthed to bring the gospel of the kingdom around the world—have we seen such hostility from the enemy.

America is not perfect. It has its problems. We have had corruption, desperation and dark times when we pulled away from God just like the spiritual walk of any human being. Unlike many nations, however, America's corruption has been hidden, and when exposed, we attempted to deal with it. Today, the light of God is shining in our nation for an awakening. Salvation begins at home. God is cleaning house!

There has never been a time of greater exposure of wickedness in our nation. The enemy wants to corrupt America. He wants to gain a foothold in America for evil and darkness. However, this only exposes his plans. We are seeing darkness exposed by light and the elements of evil are running. We are seeing all kinds of evil manifesting to keep their foothold in the nation, trying to hang on to their authority in the greatest nation in the world. By God, however, they are losing their grip on this nation as the Ekklesia is being positioned into a place of a great awakening and revival.

We must look past the surface of current events to see as God sees, to react as God reacts, to receive the manifestation of heaven that God desires on the earth.

Why are the nations in an uproar? Because change is here. I declare to you that we will see peace in this nation and the nations of the world. Chaotic times cannot remain. Almighty God is not fazed by what he sees on the news. He cares about what he sees in our hearts.

Understanding the times we are living in and having the knowledge to instruct the nation is what Issachar is about—bringing understanding, knowledge, wisdom, revelation and discernment.

Now, we understand that God is a God of judgment. He judges the wicked and the wicked are going to hell. We understand that nations are either going to be goat nations or sheep nations.

> *The wicked will return to Sheol,*
> *Even all the nations who forget God.*

> Psalm 9:17

The wicked will return to Sheol as the righteous return to God. The nations are evolving. God is bringing about his righteous judgment on the earth.

Evil will cease. Righteousness will prevail. Jesus wins. King Jesus has overcome the world and he is raising up an Ekklesia—a church that will not back down until we see the kingdoms of this world become the Kingdom of our God. As we press toward "the goal for the prize of the upward call of God in Christ Jesus," we are causing the kingdoms of this world to become the kingdoms of our God.

UNDERSTAND

Consider again the description of Issachar from 1 Chronicles 12:32

> *Of the sons of Issachar, men who understood the times*
> *with the knowledge of what Israel should do. Their*

152

chiefs were two hundred and their kinsmen were at their command.

The entire tribe was ready for action.

Let's move past our cultural and language interpretation of this word. Let's unpack it to get the stone back in place.

Consider the word *understood*. It means "an understanding," of course, but it also means: "discernment, truth, to discern, to act wisely, intelligent, to interpret, to be investigative, a skilled teacher, understanding and he will gain."

Understanding and he will gain.

With this definition, knowledge is more than just "Oh I know." Rather, we seek understanding to be able to gain, to move forward and progress the agenda of the heart of the Father throughout the earth.

The clearest meaning of *understand* is "truth." Today, truth is more detested than a lie.

Woe to those who call evil good, and good evil;
Who substitute darkness for light and light for darkness;
Who substitute bitter for sweet and sweet for bitter!

Isaiah 5:20

We are in that day right now. We have news all day long, 24/7, but little of it is truth. Instead, we are seeing reporting that seeks to change our culture, our times and the assignments that God has given us.

America is in a cultural war over revisionist history. The fact is, you cannot erase your history and correct your history at the same time. History must be learned before its lessons are clear. Erasure is ignorance. We embrace our history for what it is—a historical record of the good and the bad and everything in between—so we can move forward with healing and wisdom from God and not repeat our mistakes. To not repeat history is to know history, not erase it.

America, and the world in general, faces a rising tide of activist groups operating behind noble-sounding titles and agendas. And

153

some are noble, but many are cleverly disguised to divide and dismantle the plan and the purpose of God for America.

We need to live in truth. Jesus is truth.

> *Jesus said to him, "I am the way, and the truth, and the life; no one comes to the Father but through me."*

John 14:6

> *I have given them Your word; and the world has hated them, because they are not of the world, even as I am not of the world. I do not ask You to take them out of the world, but to keep them from the evil one. They are not of the world, even as I am not of the world. Sanctify them in the truth; Your word is truth.*

John 17:14-17

As we navigate through these times, we cannot succumb to operating in survival mode. It does no good to tread water until Jesus returns and snatches us out of here. We are an army on a battlefield—kings called to the frontlines to strategically overcome and overtake the enemy so that the Kingdom of God can be expanded around the world. Praise God.

Again, from 1 Chronicles, to "understood the times" is a powerful description. It literally means "to always have understanding." My redneck understanding would say "being in step with God or being current with him on current events."

God is speaking today. He is not silent today or any day. There is an open heaven today. We may not always hear him, but God is always talking.

When the scripture refers to "the times," it means "appointed times, circumstances, intervals, timely by year." So, it is not just the time or a season but an appointed time. We are in an appointed time—a time in our lives when we need to step up as never before. The opposition is great. Darkness is real. The enemy is in our face. But today is the day, we say: "Back off Satan, you have crossed the line."

You are from God, little children, and have overcome them; because greater is He who is in you than he who is in the world.

1 John 4:4

It is time for the Ekklesia to capitalize on this opportune time God has us in. We were born for this! Pull yourself up by your bootstraps, square your shoulders and declare: "I am ready. Here I am, God. Send me. I will be a voice. I will be the light. I will be what you need me to be to turn this nation into a place of revival and awakening."

KNOWLEDGE

The tribe of Issachar were people who "understood the times with the knowledge of what Israel should do." The word *knowledge* here is "to know, be aware, to tell, to speak, light." There was an awareness within them; it was in their DNA. They clearly understood, comprehended and made themselves known.

So, when Issachar was called upon for the nation, it was about battle. They had wisdom and understood the times—the appointed times and the circumstances they were in. Consequently, they could clearly comprehend and were able to communicate it properly.

We are looking for answers today. We are looking for insight to know what to do. We are looking for Issachars.

We live in a world where everybody tells you to love everybody. Jesus loves everybody too, right? But let's be clear. When we love people, it does not mean that we always agree with them and conform to their ideology or belief system. Relationships include disagreement, conflict and healthy tension. Rather than conforming, we stay true to who we are and we love them as God loves them without compromise. We love those who are running crazy, rioting, screaming and looting. We love those with whom we disagree. We love those who aren't like us.

We need answers. We have got to be able to comprehend.

There are various groups and organizations that are buried in their ideologies, philosophies and agendas that are wreaking havoc in our communities today. You might say, "Greg, don't you care for them? Doesn't God love them too?" You are correct-I don't hate them, and God loves them too. But these organizations and groups whose whole agenda is to pervert the truth with actions that result in crime and violence, I cannot walk hand and hand or shoulder to shoulder with them. There must be a dividing line for truth to illumine their perverted agendas.

John 8:32 says:

> *And you will know the truth and the truth will make you free.*

People must know the truth. It will make us free. That's why I am passionate about knowledge and helping people get educated on things, especially history and the Bible.

Do

The next word in this passage is *do*, meaning "to accomplish." The Issachar tribe understood present circumstances and was able, through knowledge (i.e. light), to give direction and an ability to accomplish what God wanted accomplished.

Issachar was not a tribe where you heard: "Let's have a council. Let's come together. Let's throw some ideas out here. What do you say? What's going to make you happy? Let's try to blend this together."

No. They said: "These are the times we are living in, the circumstances at hand. Here is what God is saying and here is what we must accomplish from the will and intent of God's heart, that his kingdom may come. Hallelujah."

This word *do* does not just mean "to accomplish a task or an assignment," but is also: "an awareness and a discernment to know what we need to keep and what we need to let go of."

In the church today, there are some things we need to keep and dust off, and there are some things we need to get rid of. There are

156

things we need to release from the church and repent of because they have been part of a culture that is not necessarily kingdom culture. Church culture/religious culture is not necessarily kingdom culture. We must be a people who are willing to sacrifice, lay down, release and rid ourselves of our culture when it does not line up with the culture of the Kingdom of God.

A few years back, we flew to Hilo on the Big Island in Hawaii and hailed a taxi to get to our hotel room. My wife and I got to conversing with the taxi driver who claimed to be a born-again believer. We talked about a lot of stuff until we mentioned the daily erupting of the volcano. We even felt the tremors on Oahu where we used to live for ten years. From our standpoint, we mentioned it to declare a stoppage to the eruption which was affecting hundreds of families on the island. But quite surprisingly, the taxi driver halted us, adamantly claiming that the reason the volcano is spewing lava is because "Aunty Pele was cleansing the land." My wife and I looked at each other in disbelief. How sad that a so-called Christian would have a mixture of faith, lumping together a belief in God with a false goddess like Pele. (Pele is believed to be the Hawaiian goddess of fire. They say that her body is the lava and steam that comes from the volcano.)

On another occasion, during our first Bible school graduation in Kailua Hawaii, there was a husband and wife in the class, and the wife happened to be pregnant at that time. As customary in the culture of Hawaii, everyone graduating gets a lei. As one was put around the wife's neck, the husband immediately cut the lei with scissors. Dumb-puzzled by such action, I challenged him on why he did such a thing. That's when I realized I should've waited to ask because his answer agitated me even more. He claimed that when a woman is pregnant, she should not have a lei put around her neck without cutting it first. In Hawaiian culture, they believe that it could cause the umbilical cord to wrap around the baby's neck and kill it.

Folks, we cannot mix pagan culture with kingdom culture! We must be discerners and learners of truth! Issachar's tribe understood what needed to be kept and what needed to be released. We are in that place today.

Some Churches today embrace social justice, but in so doing, they unwittingly admit sub-messages that are in stark contrast to the Spirit of God. To be clear: We raise our hands to the Lord and we kneel only before God.

Yes, when God moves, culture shifts. We don't always understand the shift. What we must discern, though, is when cultural forces are usurping the culture of the Kingdom of God. Outside agendas with no real roots in Holy Spirit will weaken and destroy us. Compromise brings us into a place where we cannot impact the world as God has ordained us to do. It can only bring inertia.

The word *do* also means "to make you ready." The words that came from Issachar readied Israel for what they would face ahead of them. We need prophetic voices today to rise up and give the Word of the Lord to make the Ekklesia ready for what God has called us to do.

> *A man takes joy in fitting reply*
> *and how good is a timely word!*

> Proverbs 15:23

Hiding in our church buildings until Jesus returns will not change the world. The tired excuse: "Well, they are just full of devils and we do not need to try to save them or minister to them or stand up for righteousness against them" isn't working either. We are called to be bold, confident confronters with kingdom mindsets and kingdom answers that bring about revival and awakening and the heart of God into the earth.

We need prophets who aren't tickling ears but prophesying the Word of the Lord. We need true apostles to rise up, come forth and decree: "This is what God is saying and this is the direction we are going." Then we will move into that direction, take ground and possess territory for the Lord. We have the knowledge to know what to do in this land.

TIME FOR KINGDOM SAKE

Time is very important. Culture is being attacked and torn apart. How do we shift culture back in the Kingdom? God is not going to do it on his own. God is not going to wave his scepter and sovereignly create a new culture. An executive order cannot do it. Legislation cannot do it. A court cannot do it...unless it comes from the courts of heaven and the Ekklesia rising up and releasing the Kingdom of God here on the earth.

We are living, in a perfect time to establish the Kingdom of God. The harvest is ripe. God is bringing things into a place that can be structured in the order of the kingdom and a harvest to be reaped. Consider the difference between religion and kingdom.

Religion sees turmoil.

Kingdom sees a harvest.

Religion says "We're losing."

Kingdom says "We're advancing."

Religion says "We have lost."

Kingdom says, "The battle is not over. God is fighting for us. It is his battle after all (2 Chronicles 20:15). We need to march forward with him."

Religion says "Darkness is taking over."

Kingdom says "Hang on."

Light dispels darkness! Darkness cannot stand light. And when the Ekklesia arises and shines brighter, darkness cannot help but flee. Dark and light do not, cannot and will not coexist! There is a great light that is appearing now. Hallelujah!

If you cannot sense the season we are in, my friend, it may be because you are doing it wrong. Life is measured by time. A life misused is time wasted. Personally and corporately, it is important to understand the time that this nation is in. Wasted time is a wasted life and a wasted nation.

Time is an interruption of infinity. God is causing us to focus on this particular time in eternity and bring solutions so eternity increases into the heart of God. Time is a brief moment in eternity with measure. When I hear the word *measure*, I think about the word *graduate*. We know that God's Word says he takes us from faith to faith and glory to glory. Symbolically, *graduate* means there is growth, an accomplishment, a measure of increase being made. The sides of a ship have a vertical row of numbers to show its depth in the water. We are in some deep water today and we need to understand how deep.

God is able to see the end from the beginning, even when we are in the middle of it. Still, our participation is crucial. When God wants to do something on the earth, he uses a man to do it. (Likewise, when Satan wants to do something on the earth, he also uses a man to do it.) God sees us where we are. He knows where he wants us to be, but there has to be an understanding of the time and a knowledge of how to navigate through the time as a nation.

Ecclesiastes 3:1 says:

> *There is an appointed time for everything.*
> *And there is a time for every event under heaven.*

We are in an appointed time. Now, some say God appointed this to be a destructive time on the earth. I do not believe that. God takes the things that the enemy meant for evil and turns them for good. We are to understand this time and steward it according to the kingdom mandate that God has given us to bring into the earth.

Time was created for purposes to be fulfilled. All of us were created for this time. This is where God's anointing and yoke-breaking purpose was meant to arise and shine.

Do not retreat!

Move forward with the word from God.

Move forward with a plan from God.

Move forward with the wisdom of God.

Time manifests itself in seasons. Issachar understood how the season had to do with the time. Everyone is born in time, but everyone must catch their season. I was born in 1968, another turbulent time in the nation, but we have to catch our season. The Issachar anointing can do this in our lives.

Life is not measured by *duration* of time, but by *donation* in time. People say "Well, I want to live to be a hundred, maybe a hundred twenty years old. I know I cannot keep all my hair, but if I could keep all my wits, I'll be all right."

What matters is not your *duration* on the earth but your *donation* in the midst of the time that God created you to function in. Rise up, come into your purpose, destiny and anointing and bring the answers of the Lord to the nations. In Jesus' name!

> *He [the enemy] will speak out against the Most High and wear down the saints of the Highest One, and he will intend to make alterations in times and in law; and they will be given into his hand for a time, times, and half a time. But the court will sit for judgment, and his dominion will be taken away, annihilated and destroyed forever. Then the sovereignty, the dominion and the greatness of all the kingdoms under the whole heaven will be given to the people of the saints of the Highest One; His kingdom will be an everlasting kingdom, and all the dominions will serve and obey Him.*

> Daniel 7:25-27

Notice what the enemy, in Daniel 7, intends to do: *alteration.* It literally means "to change, damage, pale, violate, restructure, pervert." This scripture is coming alive right now in our nation. The enemy wants to pervert our laws and time.

The word *time* in this passage: means: "appointed period, epics, definite time, ordained time and purpose."

The enemy wants to change times and laws to wipe out our history. There are those who have been elected into our government

161

on a state and federal level whose entire agenda is to shift our culture. There was a time when immigrants would come into this nation and learn to speak English. They grafted themselves into the culture of America and became Americans even while preserving their original heritage. Today, people are coming from all parts of the world and wanting to make America like the place that they left. They are attempting to change the culture.

Our nation will not survive unless the church embraces the Issachar anointing so that we understand the times and know how to bring about a righteous answer in our nation.

The enemy has had an agenda in our country going back into the 20s and the 30s. Margaret Sanger started Planned Parenthood with the agenda to annihilate the black race. She set up abortion clinics in major black metropolitan areas. Millions upon millions have been killed over the years, murdered by this woman's vision.

She also worked to destroy the family unit by pulling the man out of the home, thereby bringing the family unit into a place where it violates God's standard of a husband and a wife and children coming together as a family unit. The Ku Klux Klan was part of it. Black men were pulled from the family by being jailed for disproportionally long sentences, all to destroy our nation.

In the 1960s, atheist Madeline Murray O'Hair was determined to get prayer out of school. She succeeded and schools have never been the same.

Our education system is full of people who hate our nation. Children are not praying in school. They are not praying at home. We are seeing biblical values neglected in their education. Godly purpose is no longer there.

In the 1970s, abortion was made legal, which is another example of changing and altering our times, culture and structure, perverting these things and the plans God ordained.

The wartime spoken of in Daniel 7 literally means "a moment, a situation, a testimony to or against." How we handle time determines if it will be a testimony *for us* or *against us*. The Bible says:

> And they overcame him because of the blood of the Lamb and because of the word of their testimony, and they did not love their life even when faced with death.

Revelation 12:11

CONCLUSION

Let us take heart from the words of God to Joshua as he assumed leadership of the Nation of Israel, a divided and contentious people struggling with competing agendas and a fleeting faith in Almighty God.

> Moses My servant is dead; now therefore arise, cross this Jordan, you and all this people, to the land which I am giving to them, to the sons of Israel. Every place on which the sole of your foot treads, I have given it to you, just as I spoke to Moses. From the wilderness and this Lebanon, even as far as the great river, the river Euphrates, all the land of the Hittites, and as far as the Great Sea toward the setting of the sun will be your territory. No man will be able to stand before you all the days of your life. Just as I have been with Moses, I will be with you; I will not fail you or forsake you. Be strong and courageous, for you shall give this people possession of the land which I swore to their fathers to give them. Only be strong and very courageous; be careful to do according to all the law which Moses My servant commanded you; do not turn from it to the right or to the left, so that you may have success wherever you go.

Joshua 1:2-7

The message is clear: Do not be afraid. Be of good courage. Be of good cheer. You are going to cross over this Jordan. God is calling us into a place of courage, but it is hard to have courage if you do not understand the times, and know what to do in the midst of times.

> *Let the heavens be glad, and let the earth rejoice;*
> *And let them say among the nations, "The Lord reigns."*

1 Chronicles 16:31

Let us decree over America that we say among the nation with joy and gladness in our hearts that the Lord reigns.

> *For what great nation is there that has a god so near to*
> *it as is the Lord our God whenever we call on Him?*

Deuteronomy 4:7

God draws near to us when we draw near to God.

> *Draw near to God and He will draw near to you. Cleanse*
> *your hands, you sinners; and purify your hearts, you*
> *double-minded.*

James 4:8

When God sees a flicker in your heart in his direction, he will run to you.

> *Blessed is the nation whose God is the Lord*
> *The people whom He has chosen for His own inheritance.*

Psalm 33:12

A nation whose God is the Lord is blessed. I still believe America is a Christian nation—not a religious nation but a Christian nation, one that has kingdom purpose through the Lord God of America. Hallelujah!

The Lord will come to us and hear us when we call, for we are his inheritance. Whenever the stone of Issachar is out of place, it means there is no return for our labor. It means more people on welfare, jobs leaving for other countries and the economy suffering.

The destruction of a nation occurs from within when the Issachar stone is out of place. We are living in darkness, ignorance, believing that whatever will be will be. It defies God's purpose. A lackadaisical spirit says that whatever happens has to be sovereignly

164

ordained, that what we are seeing is God's will. This is not true; this is not how God works. Such lies cause people to withdraw and hide, weakening the church to live beneath its God-given purpose. It is the expansion of religion, not the kingdom.

We need the Issachar stone in place for the fire of God to fall on our nation and all the nations of the world, that we may know what to do in any given situation, at any given time. God is speaking; we must take heed!

THE STONE OF ZEBULUN

Commerce

WHEN ELIJAH CALLED THE PEOPLE OF ISRAEL TO HIM, he began rebuilding the altar with the twelve stones from the broken altar. The Word says that he healed and cleansed the stones before putting them in place for the fire of God to fall.

God does not pour out his Spirit just anywhere. If it randomly happens somewhere, it's strange fire. God pours out his Spirit, his fire, revival and awakening in places that are prepared to receive.

Zebulun is not mentioned a lot in preaching today, but there are over 43 references in 11 different books of the Bible about Zebulun. He represents some very important factors that we need to understand about getting him back in place.

THE WORLD

To begin with, let's look at this scripture in a new light.

> *For God so loved the world, that He gave His only begotten Son, that whoever believes in Him shall not perish, but have eternal life.*

John 3:16

This tells us that God is interested in the entirety of the world. Religion looks at this verse as positioning mankind for heaven, but the kingdom looks at it as sending Jesus to occupy the world and its systems for the Kingdom of God.

The world? Yes, the world that *God so loved.*

The word *world* in John 3:16 is the word *kosmos*, with a "k," not a "c." This word *kosmos* literally means: "system, order, governmental structure, ruling structure."

The word *world* is not the word *earth*. The Bible didn't say: "For God so loved the *earth*..." Rather: "For God so loved the *world*..." meaning: "systems, structures, mode of operation, governmental structure."

Notice that it does not say: "God so loved *humans*..." Rather, it refers specifically to the systems that God put in place.

John 3:16 is literally saying to us: "For God loved *order* so much that when things were out of order, he sent Jesus, his only begotten son, into the disorder to bring order, and those who would believe in his mission and assignment would not perish but have eternal life."

In the next verse, we see God's desire for the world that he loves.

> For God did not send the Son into the world to judge the world, but that the world might be saved through Him.

> John 3:17

Jesus was not sent into the disorder to condemn it, but that the world system—the disorder—might be saved through him.

God loves the kingdom, the governmental structure. When he orders our steps, things come into alignment with God's purposes. Paul reflects on this here:

> But all things must be done properly and in an orderly manner.

> 1 Corinthians 14:40

When the devil tempted Christ in Luke 4, he showed him all the kingdoms of the world in a moment's time. The enemy knew that Jesus' goal was the kingdom. Jesus frustrated the devil, however, because he could not get Jesus to take the bait to remain in disorder.

The original Zebulun was a unique person operating outside of the temple. He was in the world; he operated in the systems of the world, but he built the kingdom of Israel.

ZEBULUN DEFINED

Zebulun's name means: "habitation, to dwell, exalted, honor, valor, skillful in war, skillful in furnishings, gifts of endowment, able to give, great inheritance to bestow." It is from the root name *Zebul* and it means "to dwell."

Leah was Zebulun's mother. She named him this to celebrate her new son. To her, it meant that Jacob would be dwelling with her instead of being in her sister Rachel's tent.

> *Then Leah said, "God has endowed me with a good gift; now my husband will dwell with me, because I have borne him six sons." So she named him Zebulun.*

Genesis 30:20

The tribe of Zebulun was on the Mediterranean and the Sea of Galilee. The focus of the tribe of Zebulun was business and entrepreneurship, and they thrived as a major financer of the kingdom of Israel. Their finances came through ships docking at both ports. They also profited from caravans coming in and through their territory. Their symbol was a ship. Zebuluns were not bitter, angry or unjust people. They simply took what had been allotted to them by God and brought funds into the kingdom of Israel.

Today, God is redeeming business people for kingdom purposes. This is revolutionary to some people's thinking, but it began with the tribe of Zebulun many centuries ago. Still, there are many who resist this way of thinking as "too worldly."

Religion says you can go in business and give to the church for missions or a building project or to buy a new organ. But kingdom says God is building his church with a kingdom mandate that originates outside the walls of the brick and mortar mentality. God is redeeming the mountain we call business. God is redeeming the world.

Of course, not all kingdom business people are church members. That's OK. God is taking people who are in business and shifting their mindset to the kingdom anyway. Eventually, I do believe they will be born again. It's hard to hang around the King and not fall in love with him.

Kingdom Financiers

God spoke to me at 17 years old and said I was going to go to Australia and the Philippines and have great impact in those nations. Today, we are doing that. But my very first trip to Australia was not to preach a revival or seminar or teach in churches or a Bible school. No, our first trip to Australia was to do a conference for business people. That conference was called, "Kingdom Entrepreneurs." It was led by Jeremy and Emily Bell—great entrepreneurs and kingdom business people who are making a tremendous difference financially in the nation of Australia.

Jeremy and Emily, along with others, use their money to bring in internationally known speakers who move in signs and wonders and miracles and see thousands of people born again. They use their money to rent large stadiums that draw thousands of people to participate in these ministry outreaches.

That's what a kingdom business does. It understands that God has given us stewardship to advance his kingdom on the earth.

Others, like Jeff Sparkes, a friend of mine from Northlakes in Queensland, Australia, has a tremendous impact on businesses, helping proprietors get their affairs in order legally so their businesses can give into ministry without restraint. Terry Tyson is another great businessman from Colorado. He is into oil and stock investments, among other things. He is a great financier of the Kingdom of God.

Another couple in Australia, Kevin and Tracy Philippa, operates from their sole desire to fund the kingdom. They used to be pastors, but they got fed up with the traditional week-to-week grind of church minutia that seemed very religious to them. God shifted them into business and today, as they take care of people who can't take care of themselves, (the elderly and disabled) they fund the kingdom. Their business has expanded majorly as a result of sowing into other ministries.

Prosperity is when you have enough to do what God has called you to do and some leftover to help others do what God has called them to do. That's prosperity in the Kingdom of God.

God is raising up men and women like these, pouring his Spirit into their hearts and bringing them into alignment for kingdom purposes.

KINGDOM BUSINESS

Zebulun was a major financer of the Kingdom of Israel, but we'll use their example to understand where we are today in building the Kingdom of God.

In the definition of Zebulun, the words *habitation* and *dwell* mean something different than they do today. They literally mean "to occupy." The expanded definition is "to take or hold or control the enemy's troops or land." It also means "to feel or to perform the function of an office or position, to conduct business on the king's behalf." Zebulun moved in and took charge of the enemy.

Consider the parable of Luke 19. This is the story of a nobleman (a king) who goes away to reclaim a kingdom, but before he leaves, he gives his servants money to invest while he is gone.

> *A nobleman went to a distant country to receive a kingdom for himself, and then return. And he called ten of his slaves, and gave them ten minas and said to them, 'Do business with this until I come back.'*

Luke 19:12-13

The nobleman in this story went to receive a kingdom. The Greek word for kingdom is *basilia*, from the root word *basilio*. It means "royal power, sovereignty, to be king." Obviously, Jesus is speaking of himself.

The word *business* in this passage means "to busy oneself with a deed or a matter or a cause, to attend to or to collect as in to receive, to perform."

This passage is slightly different in the KJV.

> He said therefore, A certain nobleman went into a far country to receive for himself a kingdom, and to return. And he called his ten servants, and delivered them ten pounds, and said unto them, occupy till I come.

> Luke 19:12-13 KJV

Notice: *"occupy till I come."* In the KJV, the word for *business* is *occupy*. In the NASB, it translates *"do business until I come back."*

This word *business* literally means: "occupation, work, business, cattle, craftsmanship, duties to perform or performed, a messenger, an ambassador or an envoy." (Why is *cattle* part of the definition? Because cattle were the primary economic driver in those days. We might say "stocks and bonds" today.)

So *occupy* and *business* are interchangeable in scripture. They are legal terms in the Kingdom of God. Consider Psalms 107:23

> Those who go down to the sea in ships,
> Who do business on great waters.

It's talking about business. Sounds like Zebulun, doesn't it? We are doing the king's business today. What is the king's business? It's Kingdom.

God's business is kingdom, government, nations and countries. To operate as such, there must be economic engines built and running for the kingdom to thrive. This requires Zebulun people.

God is raising up people who create inventions, have a kingdom understanding and an entrepreneurial spirit. God is using them to create and distribute wealth, not in a socialism mindset but in a giving, sowing and reaping mindset. This is kingdom.

Business is a legal term, and we find it in some unexpected settings. When Jesus approached a man full of demons, the demons screamed:

And they cried out, saying, "What business do we have with each other, Son of God? Have You come here to torment us before the time?"

Matthew 8:29

These demons were asking: "What *business* do we have with you now? It's not our time to do business. Have you come to torment us before the time?"

Business is a legal transaction with accountability. When money is given for goods and services, there must be a warranty. You must guarantee some things whenever that trade is a legal transaction.

ACCOUNTABILITY

The parable in Luke 19 also gives us a greater understanding of the accountability that God expects of us. The king was generous with the first two servants but rough with the third.

When he returned, after receiving the kingdom, he ordered that these slaves, to whom he had given the money, be called to him so that he might know what <u>business</u> they had done. The first appeared, saying, 'Master, your mina has made ten minas more.' And he said to him, 'Well done, good slave, because you have been faithful in a very little thing, you are to be in authority over ten cities.' The second came, saying, 'Your mina, master, has made five minas.' And he said to him also, 'And you are to be over five cities.'

Luke 19:15-19 [emphasis added]

In verse 15, the word *business* literally means "to examine thoroughly, to gain by trading as one who has busied himself."

Notice also that the king wasn't giving out churches or ministry or money for faithfulness. Instead, he was giving authority over cities—ten of them to the first slave and five to the second. Jesus was giving us a picture of government and business being delegated to people who are faithful.

Again, this is not ministry. This is not preaching or prophesying; nothing we would call church in the conventional sense. This was a business transaction that shifted these people through faithfulness in a governmental role that enabled them to oversee business in several cities.

The third slave in the parable didn't do so well.

> *Another came, saying, 'Master, here is your mina, which I kept put away in a handkerchief; for I was afraid of you, because you are an exacting man; you take up what you did not lay down and reap what you did not sow.' He said to him, 'By your own words I will judge you, you worthless slave. Did you know that I am an exacting man, taking up what I did not lay down and reaping what I did not sow? Then why did you not put my money in the bank, and having come, I would have collected it with interest?' Then he said to the bystanders, 'Take the mina away from him and give it to the one who has the ten minas.'*

Luke 19:20-24

This hapless slave hid the king's money under the pretext of safekeeping. He was not advancing, not investing, not taking risk. He was staying "safe" until the master returned. (Probably waiting for rapture to save him.) That's not kingdom; that's a religious mindset. "You're going to have to give an account of the talent God gave you, so safeguard it!"

Religion teaches that it's about your gift, your talent and calling, that you must be faithful with it to bring a few people along with you to heaven, and then someday you'll hear God say: "Well done my good and faithful servant." Religion is wrong.

The issue is not an anointing, a gift or a talent. It's not the ability to sing or to preach or play or to give a Sunday school lesson. This is about money, business, legal accountability. This is God wanting to expand his financial interests on the earth and rule over cities.

This is what it means to do kingdom business. God gives seed to the sower and he expects an increase. If we hold back in fear, we will advance nothing. But if we reach out in faith, partnering with God (who desires to partner with us), we will prosper. The Bible tells us that God is the one who makes us wealthy. Why? So we can expand his covenant on the earth. Prosperity is a blessing.

> *It is the blessing of the Lord that makes rich,*
> *And He adds no sorrow to it.*

Proverbs 10:22

Please understand, however, that the resources God gives us are not to buy our daily bread, get us through the week or let us have a yearly vacation thrown in. That's okay too, but there's more to living than a mediocre life. God gives resources, as we steward them properly, to expand his kingdom here on earth.

This king in Luke 19 gave money and said, "Go make yourselves busy while I am restoring order to my Kingdom, and as you make yourself busy with my matters, attend to and collect those things that perform. When I return, I'm going to examine thoroughly and expect a gain from your trading as one who has been busy."

When you're faithful with a little, God will cause you to be a king over much (ref. Matthew 25:23).

CREATED ENVIRONMENT

God loves management. It started in the garden.

> *This is the account of the heavens and the earth when they were created, in the day that the Lord God made earth and heaven. Now no shrub of the field was yet on the earth, and no plant of the field had yet sprouted, for the Lord God had not sent rain upon the earth, and there was no man to cultivate the ground.*

Genesis 2:4-5

God created plants but he kept them from growing by withholding rain. Why did he do this? Because he had no man to manage the earth.

175

Then the Lord God formed man of dust from the ground, and breathed into his nostrils the breath of life; and man became a living being. The Lord God planted a garden toward the east, in Eden; and there He placed the man whom He had formed. Out of the ground the Lord God caused to grow every tree that is pleasing to the sight and good for food; the tree of life also in the midst of the garden, and the tree of the knowledge of good and evil.

Genesis 2:7-9

God created man by breathing life into him, then he placed him in the garden. Adam managed what God had given him, but it was more than a job; it was a kingdom.

Then God said, "Let Us make man in Our image, according to Our likeness; and let them rule over the fish of the sea and over the birds of the sky and over the cattle and over all the earth, and over every creeping thing that creeps on the earth."

Genesis 1:26

Some translations use *dominion* in place of *rule*. It is the word *Radha*. In the Hebrew, it means "kingdom, sovereignty on the earth." Adam had been given charge of a kingdom and God said: "I want you to do business for me. I want you to multiply. I want you to be fruitful. I want to multiply what I've given you. I don't want it to stay in this little environment, this garden that I've given you. But I want you to take what I've given you in this environment and I want you to spread it through all the earth." (ref. Genesis 1:26-30)

This is key: The word *Eden* means "presence." Rather than a location, God created an environment for Adam to flourish in. (This is why we can't find a physical Eden today. It's not a place; it's an environment that conveys a presence.)

God wants man to prosper, be fruitful and multiply in the atmosphere of *radha*, of *kingdom*. Take man out of that atmosphere, however, and he grows corrupt, bitter, angry and greedy. He kills, steals and destroys just like the god of this world. In the atmosphere of God's presence, man thrives. Outside of God's presence, man dies...slowly, imperceptibly.

The environment is crucial. Notice that God always creates the environment before he creates the subject to rule. Consider God's order of creation. Before God made fish, he made water. Before he made birds, he made sky. God made soil and then plants. God creates the environment before he creates what will occupy the environment.

If you take a tree or a plant out of the soil, its roots are exposed. There's no soil to it and so it dies. If you take a fish out of water, it will die because it's out of its God-given environment. If you take a bird out of the sky, it's vulnerable to the prey that is on the ground. The sky is the bird's protection. That's the environment where it thrives.

God created the environment for man to thrive. Zebulun thrived in this environment. He was a businessman made for the soil of entrepreneurship.

OUT OF PLACE

When the Zebulun stone is out of place, it means: "no habitation, no dwelling place, no honor for you or among you, no skill for war, no desire to fight for yourself or the king, no inheritance or endowment to complete your task."

This describes the mindset of a pauper instead of a king. It's trading for your own gain and reaping a future in outer darkness. You will not hear: *"Well done, good and faithful servant."* Greed rules your life. You're wounded. You have no scepter, no records to prove you even were in existence. You will vanish from the earth. Your name will not be remembered on the earth and your history will be erased.

That's what is happening in the nations today, especially America. The Zebulun stone is out of place and certain people are trying to erase our history. Wars are no longer fought on passion or principle. Wars are fought for finances.

We've got to understand that people aren't going to come into the Kingdom of God just because we pray. Yes, prayer is important, but there's a time to put feet to our prayers and do what God's called us to do. It starts with being sent. The Bible tells us in Romans 10:14:

> *How then will they call on Him in whom they have not believed? How will they believe in Him whom they have not heard? And how will they hear without a preacher?*

Some people consider this passage in John 2 as a counter-argument to the idea that we are to be business-minded.

> *The Passover of the Jews was near, and Jesus went up to Jerusalem. And He found in the temple those who were selling oxen and sheep and doves, and the money changers seated at their tables. And He made a scourge of cords, and drove them all out of the temple, with the sheep and the oxen; and He poured out the coins of the money changers and overturned their tables; and to those who were selling the doves He said, "Take these things away; <u>stop making My Father's house a place of business."</u>*

John 2:13-16 [emphasis added]

And yet, this passage uses a totally different word for business. In the Greek it means "emporium" or "your trading place or trading floor to merchandise a house." Jesus was saying, "You have merchandised the house of God. You have created your own trading floor. You've created your own trading place."

Jesus did not say that God was not interested in business or that business and God's house should not be connected. He said that people were not allowed to *replace* God's business with their business. God wants to be in business *with* us.

CONCLUSION

What is needed to replace the Zebulun stone? Kingdom business, kingdom entrepreneurs coming forth. God is fanning these flames. God is calling believers to the mountain of business.

From Ephraim those whose root is in Amalek came down,
Following you, Benjamin, with your peoples;
From Machir commanders came down,
And from Zebulun those who wield the staff of office.

Judges 5:14 [emphasis added]

"Those who wield the staff of office" refers to the fact that the Zebulun tribe were also rulers. The word *wield* here in the Hebrew is the word *bore*. It wasn't that they wielded it like a sword. Zebulun bore a scepter of office.

The word *office* here means: "to scribe, a writer, to steward a massive document or history, writings, books, deeds, land deeds, letters, literature, scrolls, writ."

A writ is a legal document that portrays a judgment in favor of someone or against someone. It brings the action of the court into fruition.

The tribe of Zebulun, then, were people of war, business, literature and governmental administration. Not only they were businessmen, entrepreneurs and rulers, but they were also scribes. They bore the scepter. They kept the deeds, books, letters, literature, scrolls and executed writs.

They were also fierce in battle.

> *Of Zebulun, there were 50,000 who went out in the army, who could draw up in battle formation with all kinds of weapons of war and helped David with an undivided heart.*

1 Chronicles 12:33

The Bible says that they possess all different kinds of weapons. That's important for us today.

> *For the weapons of our warfare are not of the flesh, but divinely powerful for the destruction of fortresses. We are destroying speculations and every lofty thing raised up against the knowledge of God, and we are taking every thought captive to the obedience of Christ and we*

179

are ready to punish all disobedience, whenever your obedience is complete.

2 Corinthians 10:4-6

The weapons of our warfare are not carnal—not flesh and blood—but spiritual. Why do we have these weapons? To establish the kingdom. God's given us business. God's given us the ability to war. Business people, scribes, writers, stewards of documents and executors of writ must also be able to go to war, not against each other but against the evil forces that are building up strongholds.

We need this to know this today. Greater things are coming against humanity. We have not seen the last of plagues. We will also see a great economic crisis coming into the earth. It will shift how we trade, buy and operate in an economy. This isn't necessarily a bad thing. God is tearing down one system so we can build up another—a kingdom. He's shifting us into a kingdom economic position where the king has the advantage over those who do not belong to his kingdom.

God's bringing the greatest transfer of wealth the world has ever seen. I believe it's going to be in our day and soon. God's bringing a balance and a shift in the currencies, even into gold and silver, in the way we do land and mineral rights. It will result in a great economic shift of wealth into the Kingdom of God.

When the Zebulun stone is in place, a business and entrepreneurial mantle is in operation. We become people of business who are not afraid to fight. We acquire a stewardship mantle to expand the king's affairs. We are recreated as people of honor and valor. God's people are called to rise up and be exalted by their accomplishments. It speaks of an endowment, an inheritance given for kingdom expansion, to create businesses from what passes through our land and lands on our shores.

God is restoring business into the kingdom. It's not just going to be a piece of our lives, however. For many of us, it's going to be our entire lives.

For those who have an entrepreneurial anointing and a business mind, you are called from the tribe of Zebulun to build God's kingdom. See, God didn't tell you to go to work just to make a living. He gives us resources so we can bring life, not life just to our families but life to the kingdom and our surroundings, that we cause the kingdoms of this world to become the kingdoms of our God.

Now the salvation, and the power, and the kingdom of our God and the authority of His Christ have come.

Revelation 12:10

THE STONE OF THE HOUSE OF JOSEPH

Kingship

JOSEPH WAS THE SON OF JACOB, the patriarch of one of the 12 tribes of Israel, and he had two sons, Ephraim and Manasseh, each of whom inherited half the tribe.

Joseph was Jacob's favorite son.

> *Now Israel loved Joseph more than all his sons, because he was the son of his old age; and he made him a varicolored tunic.*
>
> Genesis 37:3

Usually the firstborn is the favorite son. But Reuben sinned by sleeping with his father's wife, so he was stripped of his birthright and Joseph became the firstborn in the birthright order.

This is the blessing that Moses pronounced over the tribe of Joseph. It included Joseph's sons Manasseh and Ephraim as well because they were connected to their father.

> *Of Joseph he said,*
> *"Blessed of the Lord be his land,*
> *With the choice things of heaven, with the dew,*
> *And from the deep lying beneath,*
> *And with the choice yield of the sun,*
> *And with the choice produce of the months.*
> *And with the best things of the ancient mountains,*

And with the choice things of the everlasting hills,
And with the choice things of the earth and its fullness,
And the favor of Him who dwelt in the bush.
Let it come to the head of Joseph,
And to the crown of the head of the one distinguished among his
brothers.
As the firstborn of his ox, majesty is his,
And his horns are the horns of the wild ox;
With them he will push the peoples,
All at once, to the ends of the earth.
And those are the ten thousands of Ephraim,
And those are the thousands of Manasseh."

Deuteronomy 33:13-17

The name *Joseph* means "let him add, Jehovah has added, increase, to repeat, he is blessed and then he is blessed again, and then he is blessed again, and then he is blessed again."

You get the point. This can be summarized as "doubler." We will see how he lived out this name "doubler."

Joseph received a double portion of the inheritance of Jacob. Jacob also blessed both sons of Joseph—Manasseh and Ephraim (ref. Genesis 48 and Hebrews 11). This resulted in the two tribes coming out of Joseph, headed by his sons.

Jacob loved Joseph more than his other sons because he was the son of his old age. He gave Joseph a multi-colored tunic, making him stand out among his brothers, who grew to despise him. (The rest of the story of Joseph's turbulent upbringing is well-known.)

Jacob prophesied that Ephraim would become a greater tribe than Manasseh, even though Manasseh was the older. Thus, God upended protocol by blessing Ephraim more than he blessed Manasseh.

> *Joseph took them both, Ephraim with his right hand*
> *toward Israel's left, and Manasseh with his left hand*
> *toward Israel's right, and brought them close to him.*
> *But Israel stretched out his right hand and laid it on the*

184

head of Ephraim, who was the younger, and his left hand on Manasseh's head, crossing his hands, although Manasseh was the firstborn.

Genesis 48:13-14

This act was followed by Jacob's prophetic declaration over Joseph and his sons.

Joseph is a fruitful bough,
A fruitful bough by a spring;
Its branches run over a wall.
The archers bitterly attacked him,
And shot at him and harassed him;
But his bow remained firm,
And his arms were agile,
From the hands of the Mighty One of Jacob
(From there is the Shepherd, the Stone of Israel),
From the God of your father who helps you,
And by the Almighty who blesses you
With blessings of heaven above,
Blessings of the deep that lies beneath,
Blessings of the breasts and of the womb.
The blessings of your father
Have surpassed the blessings of my ancestors
Up to the utmost bound of the everlasting hills;
May they be on the head of Joseph,
And on the crown of the head of the one
distinguished among his brothers.

Genesis 49:22-26

At this point, the two boys were no longer just the sons of Joseph. Ephraim and Manasseh were now the sons of Jacob, who had claimed them for his own. There is a purpose for this. In the end, Jacob reached back prophetically and brought some of the blessings of Moses into a prophetic word about Joseph and his destiny.

The word *bough* in "Joseph is a fruitful bough" means "a son as a builder of the family name in the wildest sense of the word." It also means "to build up a nation or a people into a nation."

The blessings of your father
Have surpassed the blessings of my ancestors
Up to the utmost bound of the everlasting hills;
May they be on the head of Joseph,
And on the crown of the head of the one
distinguished among his brothers.

Here, Jacob is saying: "Joseph, what God is going to do in here is going to supersede where we have come thus far. You are going to have more than all of us have had together. You are going to be distinguished among your brothers and your head is a very important piece of this prophetic word."

The word *head* in the Hebrew means "rank, captain or chief." This is the same meaning as the root word of Manasseh's name. It refers to the head man of a city or nation, someone consecrated as a prince among his brothers.

This very interesting because Joseph was a dreamer, and his dreams often got him into trouble. However, it all worked out well in the end. As a prisoner in Egypt, he interpreted Pharaoh's dream when all of the other interpreters failed. Pharaoh responded by making him the number two official over the nation of Egypt (ref. Genesis 41:38-44). He literally was made to be the king in the land that he was sold to as a slave.

MANASSEH

Let's look at the root meanings of Manasseh and Ephraim. *Manasseh* means "to forget, to have a sorrowful memory or the interest of a debt evaporate, to extract one from sorrow or pain and raise them up as a chief or a captain."

Before Joseph ever got his colorful coat, before he was a dreamer or sold into slavery or went into Potiphar's house or served Pharaoh, his dad Jacob named him "chief or captain." Accordingly,

Joseph named his son Manasseh, his firstborn, "chief or captain" as well.

Joseph knew something was being lived out in his life through his son. The implication is that God gave him a son so he would be able to forget his sorrow. Gradually, the pain over how his brothers treated him evaporated. The debt that he held in his heart against them through unforgiveness gave way and the chief within him—as prophesied by his name—rose up in its place.

There is a lesson for everyone here. If we hold unforgiveness and bitterness in our lives, we will not be able to rise to the status God has for us in his kingdom. Incidentally, there is only one rank in the Kingdom of God, that of sons and daughters who are kings.

EPHRAIM

Ephraim's name means "God has made me fruitful." The word *fruitful* means "fertile." Not in the sense of "prospering in the work of my hand," but "God has enabled me to be fruitful and multiply."

The name *Ephraim* also means "to spread out" or "to declare." The sense here is a larger territory. Remarkably, the name *Ephraim* is also another name for "Bethlehem," the city that births kings.

So, we have *Joseph's* name which means "captain" or "chief." He was sent into a place ahead of Israel, and even though Pharaoh was Pharaoh, nothing happened in Egypt without Joseph's approval. Joseph was a king in Egypt.

Manasseh's name means "chief" or "captain," as well.

Finally, *Ephraim's* name means "fruitful" just like Joseph's name means "fruitful or double fruitful or doubler." And we see here that Ephraim also was another name for *Bethlehem*, which was the birthplace of the King of kings.

> *And you, Bethlehem, land of Judah,*
> *Are by no means least among the leaders of Judah;*
> *For out of you shall come forth a Ruler*
> *Who will shepherd My people Israel.*
>
> Matthew 2:6

KINGLY ANOINTING

There is a flow to the names of the House of Joseph—one of kingship, a kingly mantle and anointing.

That is what we must get back in place to see the fire of God fall, to see revival and awakening come, to see transformation and reformation come on the earth. We must get that stone back into place and step into our kingship, to that kingly mantle and that kingly anointing that God gave you and me.

Christians know that Jesus is our King, but there are many scriptures that prove to us—not only emphasize it but shout it to us—that we are kings as well. This is the intention that God had through Christ to bring us back into the governmental, kingly anointing.

What is the kingly mantle or anointing for? Why do we need it? What is it to God? Why has God called us to be Kings? Why do we need Joseph's stone back in place? And how does it affect us in our lives today when we do get this stone back in place?

I'm glad you asked. Let's start here:

> *By me kings reign,*
> *And rulers decree justice.*
> *By me princes rule, and nobles,*
> *All who judge rightly.*

Proverbs 8:15-16

> *Which He will bring about at the proper time—He who*
> *is the blessed and only Sovereign, the King of kings and*
> *Lord of lords.*

1 Timothy 6:15

Before we go further, let's establish something. Jesus is the King (capital K) of kings (small k). We are the kings—you and I. Paul, in his letter to Timothy, is talking about Jesus as the elder brother, the elder King among the family of kings, the King over kings. Scripture also refers to him as "The Lord of lords."

Some people say: "I will never be a lord." Actually, we are lords. The word *lord* is in the Hebrew word *adonai* meaning "owner." So, when we say Jesus is Lord, we are literally saying Jesus is the owner.

We know that he owns the earth.

> *The earth is the Lord's, and all it contains,*
> *The world, and those who dwell in it.*

Psalm 24:1

The owner is Adonai. God has never lost the earth. It has always remained in his hands.

This word *lord* is applied to us as well, but the application implies an owner with an emphasis on stewardship, not title or deed. The Bible tells us that God made the heavens for himself and the earth for mankind.

So, Jesus is the King of the sons of God—the kings, and he is the Lord over the sons of God—the lords. This is the partnership between heaven and earth. It restores what Adam had in the beginning, and it reactivates God's original intent of the earth.

> *And from Jesus Christ, the faithful witness, the firstborn*
> *of the dead, and the ruler of the kings of the earth. To*
> *Him who loves us and released us from our sins by His*
> *blood—and He has made us to be a kingdom, priests to*
> *His God and Father—to Him be the glory and the*
> *dominion forever and ever. Amen.*

Revelation 1:5-6

> *You have made them to be a kingdom and priests to our*
> *God; and they will reign upon the earth.*

Revelation 5:10

Notice the tense here: "You *have* made them," not "You *will* make them." This is not futuristic. It is a statement of present fact. We are what he says we are.

> *These will wage war against the Lamb, and the Lamb*
> *will overcome them, because He is Lord of lords and*

*King of kings, and those who are with Him are the called
and chosen and faithful.*

Revelation 17:14

God is calling the "chosen" and "faithful." We have a partnership with God. Jesus alone is not sweeping through the world, overcoming and conquering everything. He is fighting through our partnership with heaven. It is we who are being kings under the King and lords under the Lord. We go forth on his behalf with a kingly anointing to reform the kingdoms of this world to become the kingdoms of our God.

Even the text on his robe signifies the partnership with his family. We are a ruling family.

*And on His robe and on His thigh He has a name written,
"KING OF KINGS, AND LORD OF LORDS."*

Revelation 19:16

*I saw no temple in it, for the Lord God the Almighty and
the Lamb are its temple. And the city has no need of the
sun or of the moon to shine on it, for the glory of God
has illumined it, and its lamp is the Lamb. The nations
will walk by its light, and the kings of the earth will bring
their glory into it.*

Revelation 21:22-24

This will continue throughout eternity. Isaiah and Daniel tell us there will be no end to Jesus' government or his kingdom.

*There will be no end to the increase of
His government or of peace,
On the throne of David and over his kingdom,
To establish it and to uphold it
With justice and righteousness
From then on and forevermore.
The zeal of the Lord of hosts will accomplish this.*

Isaiah 9:7

In the days of those kings the God of heaven will set up a kingdom which will never be destroyed, and that kingdom will not be left for another people; it will crush and put an end to all these kingdoms, but it will itself endure forever.

Daniel 2:44

You are already filled, you have already become rich, you have become kings without us; and indeed, I wish that you had become kings so that we also might reign with you.

1 Corinthians 4:8

God, through Christ Jesus, has given us a kingly status in the kingdom. We are not peasants, not merely citizens or children of God. We are sons and daughters who are kings in the Kingdom of God. As such, we have authority, power, rulership, ability and responsibility.

Often, we refer to ourselves as the army of God, but this is not correct. Yes, we go to the battlefield. Yes, we war, but not as an army. The angelic host is the army of God. That is what the host means: "army."

Well...if they are the army of God, what are we?

We are kings on the battlefield. We do not go to war as privates, colonels, lieutenants or corporals, but as kings. Imagine the enemy seeing innumerable kings coming at him with kingly mantles, crowns and authority, stepping into regions, states and nations and declaring the will of the Lord. Hallelujah! Things will shift. Or as they say in heaven: "Shift happens."

That is why we have to get in place the stone of the House of Joseph. We have to realize the family of which we are a part. We are sons and daughters, kings under the King.

KINGS AND PRIESTS

But you are a chosen people, a royal priesthood, a holy nation, God's special possession, that you may declare

> *the praises of him who called you out of darkness into his wonderful light.*

> 1 Peter 2:9 NIV

In Levi, we talked about getting the priesthood stone back in place. Here, Peter is telling us that we are not just priests, but kings and priests. We are a royal priesthood, a kingdom of priests, a holy nation. Not a holy denomination, but a holy nation. We are not a religious sect on the earth. We are a government. We are a nation. We are a kingdom that comes with governmental authority and governmental power. We are the Ekklesia.

We are not beggars at the gates to the Kingdom of God, pleading: "Give us a miracle. If you see fit to do so, have mercy on us, Jesus."

No, we are stepping into the nation with heaven's authority, and we are doing it with crowns on our heads. We are God's own special people, called *"out of darkness into His marvelous light."* Light is knowledge. Darkness is ignorance. We walk in light.

When Peter says we "declare his praises," this is not speaking of a song. Rather, it refers to declaring who the King is. Make way for the King of Glory, the King of kings, after the order of Melchizedek.

Now, Melchizedek was the King of Salem, priest of the most high God. He was the king and priest who met Abraham returning from the slaughter of the kings and blessed him. In response, Abraham apportioned a tenth part of all the spoils. Melchizedek was, by the translation of his name, "King of Righteousness" and then also "King of Salem," which is "King of Peace."

Melchizedek was not just a new order of priesthood but a new order of kingship. He represented a restoration of the Kingdom of God in the earth. Many theologians believe that Melchizedek was literally Jesus.

So, why is it necessary that we are both kings and priests? Remember from our teaching in Levi that priests get things legally in

192

place through intercession, and kings operate from a place of legality (not legalism). Kings make decrees that heaven backs up because the legal standing has been established by priests.

> *I will give you the keys of the kingdom of heaven; and whatever you bind on earth shall have been bound in heaven, and whatever you loose on earth shall have been loosed in heaven.*

Matthew 16:19 NASB

Notice *"shall have been bound."* The Amplified Bible uses even stronger language:

> *I will give you the keys (authority) of the kingdom of heaven; and whatever you bind [forbid, declare to be improper and unlawful] on earth will have [already] been bound in heaven, and whatever you loose [permit, declare lawful] on earth will have [already] been loosed in heaven.*

Matthew 16:19 AMP

This is crucial. Trying to make decrees before things are legally in place is foolish and ineffective. Worse, it can be dangerous, as there can be a backlash.

When we are engaging demonic powers before legal things are in place, it gives the enemy legal right to counterattack. We can continue to pray and things can actually get worse.

Being outside of our God-ordained jurisdiction—the Greek word *metron*—removes us from the protection God has assigned to us for our assignment. God has not called us individually to conquer the entire earth. He has called the Ekklesia as a whole to go into all the earth and transform it. I do not know any apostles who are called "apostle to the entire world" today, except perhaps Jesus himself, and even he won't do it without us.

God has given us regions of influence—areas of rule. God limits us in these areas for many reasons. For starters, as we are faithful with a little, he will trust us with more. God may give us a neighborhood, a city, a nation or nations over which we have apostolic authority. Yet, when we start moving outside of our God-given realm of authority and into other neighborhoods, cities or nations, we can get backlash from the enemy. Why? Because we have stepped outside of our God-given bounds of our kingly mantle.

Paul told the Corinthians, "Look, we know our boundaries."

> *But we will not boast beyond our measure, but within the measure of the sphere which God apportioned to us as a measure, to reach even as far as you. For we are not overextending ourselves, as if we did not reach to you, for we were the first to come even as far as you in the gospel of Christ; not boasting beyond our measure, that is, in other men's labors, but with the hope that as your faith grows, we will be, within our sphere, enlarged even more by you, so as to preach the gospel even to the regions beyond you, and not to boast in what has been accomplished in the sphere of another.*

2 Corinthians 10:13-16

Our fight is not against flesh and blood but against spiritual darkness in the world that actually dwells, functions and manifests through people.

> *For our struggle is not against flesh and blood, but against the rulers, against the powers, against the world forces of this darkness, against the spiritual forces of wickedness in the heavenly places.*

Ephesians 6:12

Even though we have authority over these things, we must *know* that we are kingly and understand our apostolic authority and assigned area before we take on principalities and powers.

There are different levels of Ekklesia, each with different realms of jurisdiction. Once we as priests get things legally in place, we can take our place as kings and issue kingly decrees.

KINGLY DECREES

Let us look at some examples of kingly decrees. As you read these words, keep in mind that kingly decrees don't always translate well to language. Most decrees ROAR!

> *The Lord will go forth like a warrior,*
> *He will arouse His zeal like a man of war.*
> *He will utter a shout, yes, He will raise a war cry.*
> *He will prevail against His enemies.*
>
> Isaiah 42:13

The letters of Nehemiah's hand were also decrees of a king.

> *And I said to the king, "If it please the king, let letters be given me for the governors of the provinces beyond the River, that they may allow me to pass through until I come to Judah, and a letter to Asaph the keeper of the king's forest, that he may give me timber to make beams for the gates of the fortress which is by the temple, for the wall of the city and for the house to which I will go." And the king granted them to me because the good hand of my God was on me.*
>
> Nehemiah 2:7-8

The letters of the king to Nehemiah were decrees that opened ways for him that would not be open any other way. They gave him materials and resources to rebuild a city, a wall and his own house. The king wrote these decrees in a letter form, and because the king made a decree, all of these things were open to Nehemiah to do what he was assigned to do by God. These decrees opened up legal passage and provision.

David wrote about kingly decrees. Here, the king was the Lord.

> *It is like the dew of Hermon*
> *Coming down upon the mountains of Zion;*
> *For there the Lord commanded*
> *The blessing—life forever.*
>
> Psalm 133:3

What was the Lord's command in this passage? What was the blessing? What was the decree? *"Life forever."*

Our kingly anointing and priestly anointing are not after Levi's order; they are not even after David's order. They are after Melchizedek's order. Jesus also operates from a Melchizedek order, and he operates from the position of an endless life. *Life forever.*

Binding and loosing are also decrees. When we are binding or losing, we are releasing decrees. Such are the "keys to the kingdom."

> *I also say to you that you are Peter, and upon this rock I will build My church; and the gates of Hades will not overpower it. I will give you the keys of the kingdom of heaven; and whatever you bind on earth shall have been bound in heaven, and whatever you loose on earth shall have been loosed in heaven."*

> Matthew 16:18-19

In conferring the keys of the kingdom, Jesus was referring to kingly decrees, not merely wishful thoughts or even ardent aspirations. When you are in prayer and God directs you to address things in the authority of heaven, you are not doing it from an intercessor standpoint. You are standing in your kingly anointing with the kingly mantle of Joseph. That is what happens when the stone of the House of Joseph is back in place. That is when things change, not just for the better but with intentionality.

Let's look at the Apostle Paul decreeing a blessing over the finances of the Philippians.

> *But I have received everything in full and have an abundance; I am amply supplied, having received from Epaphroditus what you have sent, a fragrant aroma, an acceptable sacrifice, well-pleasing to God. And my God will supply all your needs according to His riches in glory in Christ Jesus.*

> Philippians 4:18-19

This was a decree made by an apostle to the Philippians, and because they had given to his apostolic ministry with such abundance, Paul was able to do all that he needed to do at that time. Their gift into an apostolic ministry enabled him to step into a realm of a decree for them. Because they gave, Paul was able to decree for God to supply all the needs in their life according to his riches.

Here are principles for making kingly decrees.

Legality. Make sure things are legally in place from your priesthood anointing.

> *But if we walk in the Light as He Himself is in the Light, we have fellowship with one another, and the blood of Jesus His Son cleanses us from all sin. If we say that we have no sin, we are deceiving ourselves and the truth is not in us. If we confess our sins, He is faithful and righteous to forgive us our sins and to cleanse us from all unrighteousness. If we say that we have not sinned, we make Him a liar and His word is not in us.*
>
> 1 John 1:7-10

Jesus' blood is the answer for everything that is out of order in your life. Sin, bitterness, unforgiveness...whatever it may be in your life, the blood of Jesus is the solution.

Be exact in your decrees.

> *As they were passing by in the morning, they saw the fig tree withered from the roots up. Being reminded, Peter said to Him, "Rabbi, look, the fig tree which You cursed has withered." And Jesus answered saying to them, "Have faith in God. Truly I say to you, whoever says to this mountain, 'Be taken up and cast into the sea,' and does not doubt in his heart, but believes that what he says is going to happen, it will be granted him.*
>
> Mark 11:20-23

Jesus was exact when he spoke to the tree and it withered up. We must believe and have a full understanding of what we are saying. We need that confidence, faith and assurance that we are speaking as representations of the King as under-kings.

<u>Believe</u> that as we are decreeing these things, they will happen. Look how Jesus did it when he rebuked the wind and the sea in Mark 4:39:

> *And He got up and rebuked the wind and said to the sea, "Hush, be still." And the wind died down and it became perfectly calm.*

Notice that Jesus did not stretch his hands over the sea and say "In the name of great Jehovah, I command thee to cease and desist, hush and be quiet."

No, he did not do that. Jesus *the man*, not *the God*, stood up to the storm and said "Hush, be still," and it was calm.

Often, Christians use the name of Jesus like a four-leaf clover or a lucky rabbit's foot, hoping that it will make what we say stick. Yet it is the anointing on our life, our aura, our persona, the presence of God with us and in us, that will establish the atmosphere of change. From our relationship with God, we can speak to things and they will align with our words.

We must not let doubt pull us out of the faith realm. From kings' decrees, we speak judgments against everything standing in the way of kingdom purpose.

Here's how Paul handled one such situation.

> *But Elymas the magician (for so his name is translated) was opposing them, seeking to turn the proconsul away from the faith. But Saul, who was also known as Paul, filled with the Holy Spirit, fixed his gaze on him, and said, "You who are full of all deceit and fraud, you son of the devil, you enemy of all righteousness, will you not cease to make crooked the straight ways of the Lord? Now, behold, the hand of the Lord is upon you, and you will be blind and not see the sun for a time." And immediately a mist and a darkness fell upon him, and*

he went about seeking those who would lead him by the hand. Then the proconsul believed when he saw what had happened, being amazed at the teaching of the Lord.

Acts 13:8-12

CONCLUSION

What are the final results when we get the stone of the House of Joseph back in place? We find ourselves on a mission, expanding the government of God into the earth as kings.

Then the seventh angel sounded; and there were loud voices in heaven, saying, "The kingdom of the world has become the kingdom of our Lord and of His Christ; and He will reign forever and ever."

Revelation 11:15

So, when the stone of the House of Joseph is out of place, what happens?

You become a destroyer of the family name in the wildest sense of the word; a destroyer of cities and nations, tearing down the ancient markers. There is no rank or honor among you and your brothers when the stone is out of place. Sadness fills your life and that piles up around you with escalating interest. Your fruit dries up and your tree stops producing. You go from the place of birthing kings to a place where kings are aborted. You begin to birth bandits and thieves.

When the stone is in place it means, "Jehovah will add to you and cause you to be an increaser." This means he will cause you to be a doubler. He will cause you to be a city builder, a nation builder, a builder of the family name in the wildest sense of the word. You will be promoted to a firstborn inheritance with the ranking of a king among your brothers and sisters. Hallelujah!

Sorrowfulness and painful memories will evaporate from your life. You will be fruitful. You will spread out. You will begin to release kingly decrees in your sphere of influence. You and your family will become known for birthing kings and producing royal priesthoods.

Are you ready? Good, because we need you.

THE STONE OF BENJAMIN

Builder

At the time of the offering of the evening sacrifice, Elijah the prophet came near and said, "O Lord, the God of Abraham, Isaac and Israel, today let it be known that You are God in Israel and that I am Your servant and I have done all these things at Your word. Answer me, O Lord, answer me, that this people may know that You, O Lord, are God, and that You have turned their heart back again."

1 Kings 18:36-37

THE ENTIRE PURPOSE OF REBUILDING THE BROKEN ALTAR and confronting the evil prophets was for the people to know that God is Lord and to turn their hearts to him.

Today, we have stepped across the threshold of a great awakening as we rebuild the altar by understanding what each stone represents. God is bringing us into a place of seeing him in a light as we have never seen him before.

Benjamin means "son of the right hand." Throughout the scripture, we see *son of the right hand* or *the right hand of God* mentioned (ref. Psalms 20). Also, in the gospels, when Jesus ascended into heaven, he sat down at the right hand of the Father. So, the right hand has significance.

We see even James' and John's mother trying to secure a place for her boys—one on the right hand of Jesus and one on the left hand (ref. Matthew 20:20-21).

The right hand speaks of authority and power. This is why a derivation of Benjamin's name is "building block, the builder of buildings" or "builder of a house."

Most often, however, the name refers not to the building itself but rather to the builder of the family who lives in the house. The word *build* is the Greek word *oikos*. It literally means "to build a house," as in a household, not a building. It means to build a family that dwells in a house, to build a lineage and to create descendants. So we have "builder of the family."

Further, we understand that "son of the right hand" refers to the one who has inheritance and goes forth and establishes the family name.

Rachel died giving birth to Benjamin, and she named him *Benoni* as she was expiring. The name means "son of sorrows" or "son of my pain." Jacob quickly changed his son's name to *Benjamin*, "the son of my right hand, the building block, the builder of the family." Fulfilling this name would be no small task.

The history of Benjamin bears this out. Benjamin was a small tribe that played an important role in the history of Israel. Like all tribes, they were godly when they lived up to their name and they were ungodly when they didn't. In fact, they were nearly wiped out through ungodliness.

It happened when Benjamin went to war against the rest of Israel to defend men in one of the cities of Benjamin who had raped a woman to death.

> *Then the tribes of Israel sent men through the entire tribe of Benjamin, saying, "What is this wickedness that has taken place among you? Now then, deliver up the men, the worthless fellows in Gibeah, that we may put them to death and remove this wickedness from Israel." But the sons of Benjamin would not listen to the voice*

of their brothers, the sons of Israel. The sons of Benjamin gathered from the cities to Gibeah, to go out to battle against the sons of Israel.

Judges 20:12-14

The sons of Israel knew there was a price to be paid to expunge such wickedness from Israel, but the tribe of Benjamin would not do that. Instead, they defended the men and found themselves in a civil war against the entire nation of Israel. Benjamin lost so badly that the entire tribe almost went extinct.

When Benjamin's stone is out of place, we experience a moral inversion. Murders are excusable, rape is an act of passion, violence is promoted, evil is called good and good is evil. We are at a place today where we have to be like the sons of Israel and say, "We will not tolerate this any longer. We will defend righteousness in the nation."

The good news is that God is raising up mature sons and daughters and five-fold ministers with backbone who are not afraid to be politically incorrect. They are not afraid of losing their jobs or careers or reputations. They are no longer focused on building a ministry or church buildings. Their focus is righteousness in the land—whatever it takes.

We cannot have any part of the spirit of religion. We must rise up and say, "We will not take part in the wickedness in the land; we will not condone wickedness. We will be like the sons of Israel. Enough is enough. No more."

We have to ask God for a day of Pentecost boldness to come upon the church again, and for us to be able to stand up and preach uncompromised righteousness. We must be a voice not only to shift the church but also to shift the nation back to its moral compass. America was founded in Judeo-Christian values. We have to get those back into that place. We have to take up the fight.

BLACK ROBE REGIMENT

During the American Revolutionary War, there was this group of ministers called the Black Robe Regiment. They were pastors and leaders of congregations who preached on Sunday. Now, they did not preach on how to better yourself, or ten steps to a better you, or estate planning with the church in mind. No, these men would pull their pistols out from under their robes, lay them on the pulpit and preach a fiery message of the Kingdom of Heaven (not hell). They would preach about current events, the war, the oppression of Great Britain, the birthing of this nation and what it would mean to generations to come.

This was especially important because, contrary to popular thinking, the colonies were divided over the issue of independence from Great Britain. Many colonials were loyal to the Crown even as their countrymen were dying for freedom.

When the Black Robe Regiment finished their sermons, these powerful preachers would put their pistols back into their holsters and lead the men of their congregations into battle. The Black Robe Regiment was feared so much that King George recruited assassins to try to kill them.

God is raising up men and women today who are not afraid to be like the Black Robe Regiment. They are taking the people of God into a direction where we are seeing reformation, awakening and God moving in power as never before.

This is not limited to America. It could be Australia, the Philippines, Hong Kong or any nation of the world. God is raising up men and women of conviction, people who do "not love their life even when faced with death" (Revelation 12:11).

BACK IN PLACE

How do we get Benjamin's stone back in place? We start by building the family. This is what God did in the garden, what Jesus came to do, and what the Father has wanted from day one. God wanted sons and daughters.

Even before the world was made, God chose us for Himself because of His love. He planned that we should be holy and without blame as He sees us. God already planned to have us as His own children. This was done by Jesus Christ. In His plan God wanted this done.

Ephesians 1:4-5

Let us look at how this unfolds as we endeavor to get Benjamin's stone back into place so the fire of God will fall and awakening will come. We are going to focus on what the name means at the root, which is to build or rebuild the family.

God blessed them; and God said to them, "Be fruitful and multiply, and fill the earth, and subdue it; and rule over the fish of the sea and over the birds of the sky and over every living thing that moves on the earth."

Genesis 1:28

God wanted a family, so he created a colony, an extension of the Kingdom of Heaven, for this family to rule. He called that colony earth. God gave mankind (Adam at Eve) two mandates:

1. Give me more family.

2. Govern, manage and steward your colony well.

Of course, they failed at governing and because of this, the family of mankind has continued to increase but without godliness. Today, both humans and the earth need to be revived, restored and reformed. They continued to have children but they lost the ability to govern when they lost their relationship with Father.

REVIVE REFORM RESTORATION

Revive

The word *revive* means "to restore life, to breath, to bring into a consciousness." When God created Adam, he breathed spirit into him and Adam became a living being. Likewise, in John 20:22, when Jesus visited his disciples after he was resurrected, *"He breathed on them and said to them, "Receive the Holy Spirit.""* The Greek wording in John 20 is the same as the Hebrew wording in Genesis 1 when God put his nostrils on Adam's nostrils and breathed life into him.

Jesus came to revive the family, (*viving*, "a bringing of life") to breathe again the breath of God into the family. When he breathes into us, it is not just to make the lungs and heart work but to put Holy Spirit back into the dwelling place that God originally intended—mankind.

Reform

The word *reform* means "to change for the better, to correct, to change in the existing form or condition of instructions and practices, to bring back to its original intent."

Reformation is from the word *diorthosis*, and its root *orthos* is where we get the word *orthopedic*. It literally means "to straighten the bone, or to bring the bone back into alignment, to level something." So, whenever we see reformation, we see *orthos* being implemented.

Adam was formed and blessed. Then he fell. God wants to bring a re-forming—a reformation—into the earth to bring his family back together again.

Restoration

The word *restoration* means "to reconstitute, a restoration or restructuring to a former condition." It is not just to change to the former position; it reconstitutes it to the former position or way that it operated.

The Father wanted family and family failed the first time. Jesus came to bring us back to the place God originally had in his heart.

THE BENJAMIN PLAN

Jesus announced his plan for restoring family:

> *I also say to you that you are Peter, and upon this rock I will build My church; and the gates of Hades will not overpower it. I will give you the keys of the kingdom of heaven; and whatever you bind on earth shall have*

been bound in heaven, and whatever you loose on earth shall have been loosed in heaven.

Matthew 16:18-19

Now, we are seeing here some very powerful words that Jesus is speaking. The King of the kingdom has come...but to do what?

He has come *to build:* the family, the family name, the heritage.

"I will build my Church." This word, *oikodomeno*, means "to build a house." Not necessarily the structure of the building but the family that resided in the building. This is what happens when the Benjamin stone is in place.

Conversely, whenever Benjamin's stone is out of place, there is destruction of the family. We see that today.

In modern times, roughly half of marriages end in divorce, Christian or non-Christian. Many children are being raised by single mothers, especially in minority neighborhoods. Indeed, our welfare system rewards single motherhood with increasing payouts for each child they have, and it penalizes people for marrying, thus excusing fathers from their responsibilities. The cycle of crime and punishment keeps women and children bound in poverty as men serve long jail sentences. Forces like pornography lure people away from their marriages with the promise of quick, easy pleasure outside the marital vows.

And this is just a sample of what happens when Benjamin's stone is out of place.

When Jesus said he would build his church, he was saying "I have come to get the family back, and Peter, because you understand that I am the Christ, the son of the living God, on this rock of revelation from the Father, I am going to rebuild. I am going to *Benjamin* my family."

In Ephesians 4, we read concerning God's gifts:

"For the equipping of the saints for the work of service, to the building up of the body of Christ."

In other words, to the *Benjamin* of the body of Christ.

207

"Until we all attain to the unity of the faith, and of the knowledge of the Son of God. To <u>a mature man</u>."

Not as babies, brats or spoiled-rotten truculents who think God is their Santa Claus, but mature sons and daughters in partnership with the Father, not only to rebuild the family but to also rebuild the family name.

"To the measure of the stature which belongs to the fullness of Christ."

These five-fold ministry gifts of Jesus are to bring the body of Christ into the full measure of the stature of Jesus Christ. Notice: full, not partial. Not a quarter. Not three quarters. Not nine tenths, but the full measure of Christ. This is what we are building. This is our family!

This is why Jesus could say: *"Greater works than these he will do, because I go to My Father"* (ref. John 14:12). We must have the five-fold anointing operating in full measure who can move and shift the Body of Christ into the full stature of the Son of God.

THE EKKLESIA

Jesus called the church *Ekklesia*. This is not a religious word but a governmental word. It finds its meaning in two different cultures— Greek and Roman.

This word *Ekklesia* in Greek culture meant, "those who gather as elders at the gate." In ancient times, the elders who gathered at the city gates were a part of an Ekklesia that governed the city. They determined what could come in the city and what needed to go out of the city.

The Romans added to the role of the Ekklesia the concept of discipling the nations that they conquered. They brought their culture, government and architecture, including their currency, to the lands they possessed, converting them to the ways of the Roman Empire. They did this through the Ekklesia, actually transplanting governing officials and citizens of Rome to these lands to rule.

This is what Jesus had in mind when he came to reestablish his kingdom government, reform its practices and restore their original form to the principles of his kingdom.

> *Go therefore and make disciples of all the nations, baptizing them in the name of the Father and the Son and the Holy Spirit, teaching them to observe all that I commanded you.*

Matthew 28: 19-20

Do we need the Ekklesia today? We have cities in crises, and legislation alone is not the answer. Even godly government leaders are not the complete answer. We need the Ekklesia to rise up and address the pervading crime, deception, poverty and oppression in our communities today. More than just gatekeepers, the Ekklesia must be culture changers determining how our cities and nations function.

God has called us to alter the culture in our cities. We are not called to coexist. We are not called to get along. We are not called to come in and just say, "Hey, we're here. If you need us, come over and we'll pray for you."

No, the calling of the sons and daughters as the Ekklesia of God on the earth is to go into cities, regions and nations and literally alter the culture to be like the Kingdom of God. That is why Jesus told us when we pray, we are to pray, *"'Your kingdom come. Your will be done, on earth as it is in heaven."* (ref. Matthew 6:10)

Jesus is telling us to bring the Kingdom of God into the earth and change the culture. However, it is one thing to know that he *said* to do it. It is an entirely different thing to know *how* to do it.

How did he tell us to do it?

He gave us instruction in two different places—the two great commissions.

TWO COMMISSIONS

> *He said to them, "Go into all the world and preach the gospel to all creation. He who has believed and has*

been baptized shall be saved; but he who has disbelieved shall be condemned. These signs will accompany those who have believed: in My name they will cast out demons, they will speak with new tongues; they will pick up serpents, and if they drink any deadly poison, it will not hurt them; they will lay hands on the sick, and they will recover."

Mark 16:15-18

In Mark 16, Jesus commissioned his disciples—and he is commissioning us today—that our first commission is to restore the family, to get it back.

How do we do that?

"Go and preach the gospel of the kingdom." Notice he never told us to go preach a gospel of salvation or prosperity or deliverance. He did not say even preach a gospel of healing. He said, "Go preach the gospel of the kingdom"-the King and his dominion.

When John was baptizing in the Jordan, he was baptizing Jews, saying, *"Repent, for the kingdom of heaven is at hand"* (ref. Matthew 4:17). And as they were baptized, they were literally changing the way they related to God.

Then along came Jesus.

Then Jesus came from Galilee to the Jordan to be baptized by John. But John tried to deter him, saying, "I need to be baptized by you, and do you come to me?" Jesus replied, "Let it be so now; it is proper for us to do this to fulfill all righteousness." Then John consented.
As soon as Jesus was baptized, he went up out of the water. At that moment heaven was opened, and he saw the Spirit of God descending like a dove and alighting on him. And a voice from heaven said, "This is my Son, whom I love; with him I am well pleased."

Matthew 3:13-17

When Jesus was baptized, he reinforced the message of the Kingdom. That is why he says in Mark 16, that when people believe that message and are baptized (Jesus' baptism by John into the message of the Kingdom), certain signs will accompany those who believe.

Jesus did not say to be born again for a long time, or go to Bible college and get a seminary degree. No. Simply be born again and signs and wonders and miracles will follow you.

Matthew 28 was a different commission.

> *And Jesus came up and spoke to them, saying, "All authority has been given to Me in heaven and on earth. Go therefore and make disciples of all the nations, baptizing them in the name of the Father and the Son and the Holy Spirit, teaching them to observe all that I commanded you;*

> Matthew 28:18-20

Notice that in Mark 16, Jesus commissioned us to revive people by breathing life into them through a personal relationship with Jesus Christ—being born-again. Yet in Matthew 28, Jesus commissioned us to disciple nations. God formed what he wanted his kingdom to be like in the earth and told us, through Jesus, to go and reform the earth.

The breadth and depth of Jesus' commissions cannot be understated. We are not to scare people into heaven. Neither are we to mend wounds and mop brows. We are to revive the lost and disciple nations, not just bring them to the cross but bring them to the resurrection. Our evangelism is to tell people about the King and his kingdom to get them to change their citizenship, to be born again. It is about getting the purpose of God in them and through them in the earth.

In Matthew 28, Jesus gave us the authority to rule and reform, and we need it. America needs reforming; Australia needs reforming, the Philippines needs reforming; anywhere where you see religion in charge needs reforming.

To effectively carry out our calling of God, we have to get both commissions right—Mark 16 *and* Matthew 28. We can preach the people in and get them baptized, but we must also disciple nations.

God is raising up people today to reform the mountains of influence: media, government, education, economy, religion, family and arts. Studies tell us that six percent of people in any industry or sphere of society lead it. So be a six percenter and change culture.

REVIVAL AND REFORMATION

We need times of refreshing, as we read in Acts 3:

> *Therefore repent and return, so that your sins may be wiped away, in order that times of refreshing may come from the presence of the Lord; and that He may send Jesus, the Christ appointed for you, whom heaven must receive until the period of restoration of all things about which God spoke by the mouth of His holy prophets from ancient time.*

Acts 3:19-21

Notice what this does not say. It does not say "Hang on. Jesus is coming to rapture you out of this mess." No. It says that heaven must receive Jesus until the period of restoration of all things.

Anapsuxis is the Greek word *breath,* meaning "times of refreshing," as when the presence of God revives us.

*Apokatastasi*s is the word *reconstitute,* "to reform." When we see refreshing and reforming, we call this *revival,* "an awakening, an outpouring, reformation and transformation." So, God's heart is not only to see revival and awakening but also reformation and transformation.

Revival stirs people up; it is an awakening. But reformation is discipling that actually changes substance. Lasting change comes from reformation, but reformation does not come without revival. Why? Because you cannot reform people groups and systems when they are dead.

America in the '60s was a time of great upheaval. Culture changed on many levels and on many mountains of influence. The change was often radical but not always for the good.

In the church, we had a revival called "the Jesus Movement." Comprised mostly of hippies, this was a non-religious awakening that incorporated many elements of hippie culture—popular music, dancing, free-flowing praise and worship, and a deemphasis of societal norms such as dress codes and respect for tradition. Suddenly, Jesus was everybody's friend and all believers were brothers and sisters. Many people came to know the Lord in those days, including several prominent ministers today. It was revival at its best.

Unfortunately, these people did not look like your Sunday morning church folks. They had long hair, lacked basic hygiene and had issues with authority. Not surprisingly, the prevailing church rejected them, so new churches were created out of the Jesus Movement by the hippies themselves, and the result was a fundamental shift in how we do church gatherings today. They completely changed church culture to suit their spiritual needs and experiences. New church movements like the Vineyard and the Charismatic churches represent some of the greatest moves of God in recent times. Their impact has been felt throughout Christendom.

Theirs was a true culture change...yet it only changed culture within the four walls of the church. We completely missed changing the culture beyond the church by impacting the systems of the world. Life within the church was good. Life outside the church was horrible. We were excellent in executing Mark 16 (revival); we failed miserably implementing Matthew 28 (reforming). As a result, we only did half of what we were supposed to do. We were supposed to disciple the world; we only discipled ourselves.

On a separate front, leaders like Dr. Martin Luther King Jr. and Malcolm X, and politicians like Hubert Humphrey and Lyndon Johnson, were changing American culture by reviving the nation's black population through a drive for civil rights, often in the face of fierce hostility.

While the assertion of civil rights brought a much-needed change in culture, the shift also had an unfortunate impact on minority communities. The same people groups that were delivered from oppression and given important rights soon found themselves in greater bondage to government welfare programs. The government basically paid them to have children and further, penalized them if the father of the children (or any adult male) was present in the home. This destroyed families, replacing the bondage of systemic racism and poverty with dependence on welfare. Racial stereotypes were furthered and generational poverty and the ensuing crime waves become entrenched in this new cultural mindset.

Further, social groups demanded that certain races vote for their political parties or be ostracized. Those same parties also demanded the right to kill their unborn babies.

Margaret Sanger, who established abortion clinics throughout the country, is celebrated as a liberator. Yet she was a racist determined to annihilate the black population in America through the aborting of black babies.

Atheists such as Madalyn Murray O'Hair fought successfully to remove prayer and Bible reading from public schools, and schools have never been the same.

Today, in large portions of our culture, the so-called "woman's right to choose" is heralded as a strident act of freedom over male-dominated oppression. Likewise, atheism is in vogue among intellectuals and young people. In the true sense of culture change, the people who champion abortion or atheism no longer question the underlying concepts behind the slogans that convey these popular positions. They simply accept them as part of modern life along with the air they breathe, the internet they absorb, the insignificance of the church and the murder of the unborn as a form of birth control.

Yes, people groups obtained rights and freedoms that they never had before, but they were being discipled by the world, not by the church, not by the Ekklesia. And so, through these initial rights and freedoms there came much bondage.

Both God and the enemy know that permanent change starts with revival but finishes with reformation—a culture shift. Our battle, then, is to withstand the culture change of the enemy and establish the Kingdom of God—a culture change bringing the government of heaven.

We awaken and revive per Mark 16, but we disciple and reform per Matthew 28. We cannot do one without the other. We have got to do both if we are going to see the power of God manifest to the level of Jesus' prayer in Matthew 6:10.

This is what it looks like with the Benjamin stone put back in place—getting the family back and reestablishing the culture of the Kingdom of Heaven in the world.

> *[Having] been built on the foundation of the apostles and prophets, Christ Jesus Himself being the corner stone,*
>
> Ephesians 2:20

The family is being fitted together, growing into a holy temple in the Lord. We are the temple of the Holy Spirit. We are being *Benjamin*—being built together into a dwelling of God.

CONCLUSION

What does it look like when the family is restored to a place of governing?

> *Also the foreigners who join themselves to the Lord, to minister to Him, and to love the name of the Lord, to be His servants, every one who keeps from profaning the sabbath and holds fast My covenant;*
> *Even those I will bring to My holy mountain and make them joyful in My house of prayer. Their burnt offerings and their sacrifices will be acceptable on My altar; For*

My house will be called a house of prayer for all the peoples.

Isaiah 56:6-7

When the Benjamin stone is in place, we have both the Mark 16 commission and the Matthew 28 commission. The family aspect and the governing aspect combine to create revival and awakening, then reformation and transformation.

When we are rebuilding the family, it is family-centered and people-centered. When we are operating as Ekklesia, it is government-centered and Kingdom-centered.

Remember that the word *build* is the Greek word *oikos* "builder of a family." We can contrast this with Ekklesia—God's legislative body—and how each carries out the commissions of Jesus.

The Oikos saves people as individuals.

The Ekklesia saves nations.

The Oikos heals people.

The Ekklesia heals nations.

The Oikos delivers from demons.

The Ekklesia delivers from philosophy, laws, structures, paradigms and systems.

The Oikos takes the love of Christ to an individual.

The Ekklesia takes the principles and commandments of God to societies and nations.

The Oikos is a household.

The Ekklesia is a Congress.

The Oikos is a flock of sheep.

The Ekklesia is a convention of Eagles.

The Oikos is a bride.

The Ekklesia is a government.

The Oikos is his body, his family.

The Ekklesia is his voice.

The Oikos is the children of God.

The Ekklesia, they are sons and daughters of God.

The Oikos are heirs of God.

The Ekklesia are partners with God.

The Oikos are farmers.

The Ekklesia are judges.

The Oikos are priests.

The Ekklesia are kings.

The Oikos are administrators.

The Ekklesia are legislators.

The Oikos are anointed for the work.

The Ekklesia is authorized for the work.

The Oikos preach Mark 16.

The Ekklesia disciple according to Matthew 28.

The Oikos performs works.

The Ekklesia they command laws and principles and ways.

The Oikos emphasizes the outpouring of the Holy Spirit.

The Ekklesia emphasizes the commands of King Jesus.

The Oikos, his spirit poured out.

The Ekklesia, his truth emphasized and taught.

The Oikos is signs, miracles and wonders.

The Ekklesia is systems and procedures.

The Oikos is power needed.

The Ekklesia is authority exercised.

The Oikos is outpouring.

The Ekklesia is out working.

The Oikos is short term.

The Ekklesia is long term.

The Oikos is pastoral and evangelistic centered.

The Ekklesia is apostolic and prophetic centered.

Both the Oikos and the Ekklesia need the function of the teacher.

The Oikos gives birth to kids and children.

The Ekklesia commissioned kings and legislatures.

The Oikos protects the family and the flock.

The Ekklesia demands risks from you.

The Oikos is about prayer.

The Ekklesia is about decrees.

The Oikos is about gathering people into the sheep pen.

The Ekklesia is about sending people into the world.

The Oikos' goal is the wholeness of individuals.

The Ekklesia's goal is the mission and the will of the King.

The Oikos gifts of the Holy Spirit.

The Ekklesia keys to the kingdom.

The Oikos releases mercy.

The Ekklesia releases justice.

The Oikos extends grace.

The Ekklesia functions in truth.

The Oikos driven by passion.

The Ekklesia driven by zeal.

The Oikos we lay hands on people to heal them.

The Ekklesia we lay hands on people to commission them.

The Oikos is where revival happens. This is where Jesus is the shepherd, the groom, an elder, the firstborn of many brethren, a high priest, a savior, a lamb, a redeemer, an advocate, a mediator, a friend, a pastor, a provider, a healer, the son of man.

The Ekklesia is where reformation happens. This is where Jesus is King, Lord, Master, Commander in Chief, Head of the Church, the Apostle, the Bishop, the Judge, the Law giver, the Victor, the Savior, the Lord Sabaoth, Captain of the Lord's host, the Word of God, the Creator, the Son of God.

These are things that happen when the stone of Benjamin is in place.

Family, we have to get out of this religious mentality that our job as the church is to get people to heaven. That is a wrong focus. We have to get the family back to govern. Certainly, if some of the family dies before the Lord returns, they will go to heaven, but Jesus never told us heaven is our focus. He said earth is our focus. Here is where our gifts are needed. Here is where the family needs revised and reformed. Here is where the governing takes place. We must get back into both of these commissions of God—Mark 16 and Matthew 28. We are going to get the Benjamin stone back in place so it can begin to bring about an awakening from the fire of God falling like God intends for us to do.

Are you ready? Let's do this!

CONCLUSION

IT STARTED WITH WATER, OR A LACK THEREOF. Two men, Ahab and Obadiah, were searching for the man they thought could end the drought that had plagued Israel for three and a half years. He was the same man who had instigated it. That man was Elijah the prophet, and he was hard to find.

So, they split the kingdom between them and looked in every city, every field and mountain. When Obadiah finally found Elijah, he was desperate to be seen as one of the good guys. Being a prophet of God in those days meant there was a price on your head. Ahab's wife, Jezebel, killed all she could find. Yet Obadiah feared God and was quick to set himself apart from the murderous witch.

> Has it not been told to my master what I did when Jezebel killed the prophets of the Lord, that I hid a hundred prophets of the Lord by fifties in a cave, and provided them with bread and water?

> 1 Kings 18:13

Obadiah needed Elijah's favor. He was afraid Ahab would kill him if he reported back to Ahab and Elijah didn't show for the arranged meeting. True to his word, however, Elijah did appear and the following conversation ensued:

> When Ahab saw Elijah, Ahab said to him, "Is this you, you troubler of Israel?"

> He said, "I [Elijah] have not troubled Israel, but you and your father's house have, because you have forsaken the commandments of the Lord and you have followed the Baals. Now then send and gather to me all Israel at Mount Carmel, together with 450 prophets of Baal and

221

> *400 prophets of the Asherah, who eat at Jezebel's table."*

1 Kings 18:17-19

So, it was going to be 850 bloodthirsty prophets of evil against one man of God. At stake was the nation of Israel.

Elijah's choice of Mount Carmel for this contest was telling. The word *carmel* means vineyard. So Elijah was saying "Meet me in the vineyard." But not just any vineyard. In the New Testament, we learn who the husbandman of the vineyard is—Father God. So this showdown was happening in God's fruitful place. And God was readying a harvest.

Elijah chose a place where God had proven himself fruitful in the past. In essence, he was saying: "Join me there and see which god answers by fire. If your god can override what my god (Yahweh/Jehovah) is doing, then we will serve Baal. But if Baal cannot come into God's mountain of fruitfulness—a place where God has a history, a present and a future—then you guys are done and we will kill you."

Sounds fair, right?

Studying the 12 stones of the altar that represented the 12 tribes of Israel, the names of several including the meaning "fruitful." The tribes of Joseph, Gad, Judah, Levi, and even Manassas and Ephraim all mean "fruitful."

What does fruitful mean? We draw fruitfulness from planting a seed. We do so in faith, believing God that the ground and rain and sunshine will do what they're supposed to do, and that inside that seed, there is not just a tree but orchards. This is the faith Elijah had. God had proven himself to Elijah many times on Mount Carmel. In issuing his challenge, then, Elijah was drawing on his history with God—the voice of God that had spoken to him in the past, the faithfulness of God that had delivered and sustained him many times. As he drew on these things, he knew that God would do these very things again.

It was the same faith David had when he took his staff in hand and charged Goliath at a dead run. The staff was a diary of sorts; in it were carved memorials to God's power to deliver and heal, the history of generations.

Elijah was declaring: "Meet me at a place where I have a history with God."

Today, when we pray for revival, awakening, transformation and reformation in our nations, we are not asking God to do something new. We are asking God to do it again. See, there have been great awakenings in America going back in the 1600s. There was also one in the 1800s. We are getting ready to see another great awakening like never before. How do I know? Because this nation has a history with God.

Certainly, not all of our history is good, but God is in our history, forgiving our failures, shortcomings and faults as we repent. Then God heals our land and brings us into a place of revival. The truth is, we have a great history with God. There have been moves of God with signs and wonders and miracles throughout our nation. Prayers have been answered. Covenants have been made. And lives have changed.

Our history with God says he is faithful to give us revival, awakening, and to pour himself out in greater ways than ever before. We are at that place in history, pulling on what God has done for us in the past and believing him to bring us into another revival.

"Meet me in the vineyard where I have met with God and he has proven himself faithful." Elijah was ready; God was ready; but were the people ready?

> *Elijah came near to all the people and said, "How long will you hesitate between two opinions? If the Lord is God, follow Him; but if Baal, follow him." But the people did not answer him a word.*
>
> 1 Kings 18:21

The people on the scene were silent. They knew their history with God, how he brought them out of Egypt and into the promised land, but they also understood there was something in this moment that could change everything. That is why they gave their water— that precious commodity in a long drought.

Elijah drew the people near and repaired the altar of the Lord which had been torn down by the prophets of Baal. Elijah took 12 stones and rebuilt the altar in the name of the Lord. Then he made a trench around the altar large enough to hold two measures of seed. He arranged the wood and cut the ox to pieces and laid it on the wood. Finally, he commanded the people to drench the altar with water, not once but three times, until water was spilling into the trench.

Then the moment of truth:

> At the time of the offering of the evening sacrifice, Elijah the prophet came near and said, "O Lord, the God of Abraham, Isaac and Israel, today let it be known that You are God in Israel and that I am Your servant and I have done all these things at Your word. Answer me, O Lord, answer me, that this people may know that You, O Lord, are God, and that You have turned their heart back again." Then the fire of the Lord fell and consumed the burnt offering and the wood and the stones and the dust, and licked up the water that was in the trench. When all the people saw it, they fell on their faces; and they said, "The Lord, He is God; the Lord, He is God."

I Kings 18:36-39

When the fire fell, the people's hearts turned and they begin to worship. Yet as spectacular as that was, it was not enough. Yes, the people were revived, even converted. But Elijah knew that the shift needed to move from the mountaintop to deep within the people's hearts. Something more had to happen to secure what God was doing in the land of Israel and her people. It was about to get real.

Then Elijah said to [the people], "Seize the prophets of Baal; do not let one of them escape." So they seized them; and Elijah brought them down to the brook Kishon, and slew them there.

1 Kings 18:40

Now, the *brook Kishon* means: "to lay bait or lure." It was at this point that God, through Elijah, revealed his end game. He had lured the prophets of Baal to their destruction. The goal of the altar was not just for the people to say, *"The Lord! He is God"* The goal was to empty the land of the prophets of Baal and the prophets eating at Jezebel's table. That remains God's strategy today.

If we are going to see a sustainable revival, not only must we revive the people through the Mark 16 commission, but we must disciple the nations through the Matthew 28 commission. We are not just getting people to a place where they say "God is the Lord." That's a good start, but we have to move outside the four walls of the church and engage culture in a way that we remove the prophets of Baal and the prophets that eat at Jezebel's table. We must get them out of the land and mute their voices of influence. Then we replace them with mature sons and daughters who speak for God, do kingdom business and are kingdom people.

We are reclaiming culture, laying traps according to God's strategy to expose the satanic systems of the world for what they are: dark, weak, worthless, self-centered and lacking the hearts of the people. We will see culture re-established as God has designed it for the nations of the world.

Now, Elijah slaughtered the prophets of Baal. We are not doing that in the natural. Instead, we are bringing a slaughter to the systems in the spiritual realm and removing those people in the natural who have held authority in our culture and turned it over to Baal. Their day is over; their realm is done. We are reclaiming the mountains of culture and influence. We are raising up people and sending them into these places to reclaim those mountains for the Lord.

Now, at this point in the story, the fire has fallen, the people have been revived, and the land has been cleansed of the evil prophets. It's time for God to restore the land.

> *Now Elijah said to Ahab, "Go up, eat and drink; for there is the sound of the roar of a heavy shower." So Ahab went up to eat and drink.*
>
> *But Elijah went up to the top of Carmel; and he crouched down on the earth and put his face between his knees. He said to his servant, "Go up now, look toward the sea."*
>
> *So he went up and looked and said, "There is nothing." And he said, "Go back" seven times. It came about at the seventh time, that he said, "Behold, a cloud as small as a man's hand is coming up from the sea."*
>
> *And he said, "Go up, say to Ahab, 'Prepare your chariot and go down, so that the heavy shower does not stop you.'"*
>
> *In a little while the sky grew black with clouds and wind, and there was a heavy shower. And Ahab rode and went to Jezreel. Then the hand of the Lord was on Elijah, and he girded up his loins and outran Ahab to Jezreel.*
>
> 1 Kings 18:41-42

"The sound of a roar." *Roar* is the word *hamon*, meaning "great quantity coming, hordes of rain coming, multitudes of rain coming, coming with a noise, a rumbling, a stirring, rain that is producing."

That's a lot of rain.

We are in the Roaring 20s, a season of the roar of the Lion of Judah over his church, his Ekklesia and the nations of the earth. Rain is coming, a time of refreshing, an outpouring of Holy Spirit as never before. Cultures will shift back into what God intended for it to be from the beginning, just as in Elijah's day.

Notice, however, the different approaches of the two men after God moved on Mount Carmel. Ahab went up to eat and drink, but Elijah crouched down and put his face between his knees. This was a position of birthing, and he was birthing rain. One man satisfied his desire; the other man continued God's restoration of the land.

This is a lesson for us today. While others enjoy the immediate blessings of God after a miracle, the Ekklesia—God's legislative arm in the earth—may find ourselves in a position of birthing the outpouring of Holy Spirit, the heavenly drenching of God on the earth. If we are going to not only hear about the rain but experience the rain, we need to birth it. Yet there is something more.

As Elijah birthed the rain, his servant finally saw something Israel hadn't see in three and a half years of drought—a cloud the size of a man's hand. An inauspicious start, but still... a beginning.

The word for hand is *cafa,* and it means "hollow, flat." So it was not a ball of cloud floating through the air with the potential to unleash torrents of rain. No, this was a flat cloud that looked hollow; you could see through it. It was like the palm of a hand. Yet it held promise. After three and a half years, Israel had a promise the size of a man's hand.

This is how God works. The people saw the fire fall, the water consumed, the altar scorched and the resident evil slaughtered in flesh and spirit. And now, at the grand moment of restoration, there arises a flat little hollow cloud. No lightning, no thunder, no dark foreboding skies. Just a puff of white. I can imagine the people thinking:

"That's going to restore the land? Gee God, did you run out of all the big stuff?"

That wasn't Elijah's thinking, however. He knew what was coming. It was being birthed through him.

"Go up, say to Ahab, 'Prepare your chariot and go down, so that the heavy shower does not stop you.'" 1 Kings 18:44

To people of faith, it doesn't matter what the cloud looks like; we are birthing rain. Can you imagine Mary looking at the newborn Jesus in her arms? A tiny, helpless infant who can't feed himself, hold himself upright or speak. This is what the angel foretold? The prophets declared? The Son of God, Savior of the world?

Yes... he is.

> Do not despise these small beginnings, for the Lord rejoices to see the work begin...

Zachariah 4:10

Every move of God starts with birth. We are birthing something today. It is no small thing when the God of all Creation whispers "I am here." Do we really need more?

When we believe what God says, regardless of our expectations of grandeur, he does more just as he did for Elijah. In a little while, the sky grew black with clouds and winds picked up and the sky erupted with heavy rain. Finally, proper rain... *after* Elijah birthed it.

This is what it means to us today: the awakening, the revival, the redemption. Our end goal is not the reassembling of stones or understanding what they all mean. Don't confuse the process with the prize. We are getting things in order to rid the land of the influence of Baal and Jezebel so the rain can fall. Not the fire—that's just a means to an end—but the rain. Fire purges but rain heals.

We are to become involved in every aspect of society, raising people up and sending them into the mountains of society to be a voice of the Kingdom of God. Baal's voice has been strong, but when all is done and we remove his prophets, our next step is to birth another voice in the land—the voice of the kingdom and the King.

The Ekklesia is bringing heaven to Earth, decreeing the heart of the Father's will, declaring, prophesying and releasing God's voice, birthing what he has given us—things we have not seen for years, some of it not since the 1800s, things long absent from our cultures.

Birthing yields small things at first. Don't despise it! Don't get talked out of it. Good things start small and grow. We must steward our nascent beginnings from the vineyard, drawing on our fruitful history with God. Then we will see clouds and rain and the outpouring of Holy Spirit.

It's not going to happen through our preaching, our theology or our talents. It is going to happen through the sons and daughters of God being led by the Spirit of God. It will be the government of heaven. As we are obedient to follow him, we will see the goodness of the Lord in the land of the living.

We will see America become what she is called to be. We will see Australia become what she is called to be. We will see the Philippines, Korea, Hong Kong, and all the nations of the earth becoming what they are called to be. To see this, we must disciple the nations of the world. We must steward culture in a way that we do not give Baal and Jezebel position and voice again any longer.

Jesus is returning for a church without spot or wrinkle, not a scared little church hiding behind walls and praying: "Come quickly, Lord Jesus. Save us from this turmoil and snatch us out of here to watch you do it all from the clouds."

No! God is saying: "Gird up your loins. Put on your signet ring. Straighten your crown. And get out there in Jesus' name. Release my decrees and prophetic words. Bring the earth back into alignment. You will not do this as a flock of quivering sheep but boldly out of your anointing as kings and the call I have given you."

Naturally, some of us hesitate. After all, doesn't scripture say *"Count the cost"*? Sure, it does. So, count. And when you get to "everything," prepare to move out.

Some people hesitate to run for a government office because there's so much evil present. Others hesitate to start teaching until God cleans up the mess of political correctness and rebellion that is rotting our educational system. Still others dream of breaking into Hollywood, but... you know... all that sin and decadence. Ugh.

Hear the word of the Lord: The reason we should be at the top of those mountains is precisely because they are so wicked. Just as the police go to where crime is and doctors go to where disease is, the Ekklesia go to where sin and darkness is.

We are awakening, reviving, and God wants to use us in mighty ways to bring about an outpouring of his Spirit like never before. But first, find your tribe!

Where do you belong? Are you a visionary like Reuben? A listener like Simeon? Knowledgeable like Issachar? A business person like Zebulun? A builder like Benjamin? A wrestler like Naphtali? A priest like Levi (but of the order of Melchizedek)? Find your place in this altar of God. We need you.

We need you where God has called you to be. We are doing business on King Jesus' behalf until he slips in on us like a thief in the night.

We are facing a tremendous opportunity to bring revival, awakening and redemption to the world. I believe a billion souls will come into the Kingdom of God in this next decade, more than have been saved in the last 2000 years.

To do this, we must function as we have never done before. We must own it. We must be it. We must steward it. We must operate from a place not just of fruitfulness for a season but of transformation for generations to come. It is they who will take it even deeper.

God is transforming the nations of the earth, and he is doing it through us.

> *He made known to us the mystery of His will, according to His kind intention which He purposed in Him with a view to an administration suitable to the fullness of the times, that is, the summing up of all things in Christ, things in the heavens and things on the earth.*
>
> Ephesians 1:9-10

Wallace:

*I am William Wallace
and I see a whole army of my countrymen,
here, in defiance of Tyranny.
You've come to fight as free men,
and free men you are.
What will you do without freedom?
Will you fight?*

Soldiers:

*Fight? Against that? No!
We will run! And we will live.*

Wallace:

*Aye. Fight and you may die. Run, and you'll live...at least a while.
And dying in your beds, many years from now,
would you be willing to trade all the days,
from this day to that,
for one chance
just one chance
to come back here and tell our enemies
that they may take our lives
BUT THEY'LL NEVER TAKE OUR FREEDOM!*

Braveheart (1995)

ABOUT THE AUTHOR

GREG HOOD WAS BORN AND RAISED IN AMORY, MISSISSIPPI, and has been in ministry for over 33 years. He is the President and Founder of Global Reformation Ministries and World Mission Center Fellowship of Churches based in the United States of America.

Greg apostolically leads many leaders and churches around the globe. He is a church planter and has pioneered several churches within the United States and in other parts of the globe. Greg travels extensively, empowering believers for the passionate pursuit of their God-given mandate, resulting in personal and societal transformation. His greatest passion is to see the Body of Christ come to its fullness. Greg is driven with great passion to speak into those who are called into leadership to the Church, Government and the Marketplace. He burns to see people become who God has fashioned them to be.

Greg and his wife Joan, have been married for 23 years. After finishing an assignment in Hawaii for ten years, the Hoods recently based their ministry back to Amory, Mississippi and have recently begun co-leading Global Connexions, located on the beautiful sunshine coast of Queensland, Australia.

Made in USA - Kendallville, IN
1177110_9781735768106
10.19.2020 1600